IRRATIONAL
INSTITUTIONS

Business, Its Leaders, and
The Lean Movement

BOB EMILIANI, PH.D.

Irrational Institutions: Business, Its Leaders, and The Lean Movement / Bob Emiliani

Cover design by Bob Emiliani

ISBN-13: 978-1-7320191-1-9
Library of Congress Control Number: 2019921262

1. Business 2. Economics 3. Leadership 4. Management 5. Sociology 6. Aesthetics

First Edition: January 2020

Published by Cubic LLC, South Kingstown, Rhode Island, USA

This publication is believed to provide accurate information with respect to the subject matter covered. It is sold with the understanding that it does not in any way represent legal, financial, business, consulting, or other professional service.

Manufactured using digital print-on-demand technology.

CONTENTS

I would like to thank readers for
their interest in my work.

Preface

Beginning around 1994, I took on a challenge to understand Toyota's management system and its derivate, Lean management. My specific interest was the leadership and management thinking and practices that enabled one to succeed in transforming an organization from classical management to Lean management. During the 14-year period through 2008, I studied these two related forms of progressive management through personal practice, observation, teaching, executive training, reading, and critical analysis. This culminated in three books and a dozen academic journal papers whose focus was principally an examination of success factors – what leaders do to achieve a so-called "Lean transformation" that sets them on path that models the success of Toyota Motor Corporation (see Note 1).

During the same period, it was apparent that some leaders who were trained in progressive management embraced it while most others did not. Specifically, this meant leaders who embraced progressive management start the process of learning to think and act in ways that were substantially different than they were accustomed to in traditional (classical) management. Some leaders were energized by this challenge, while most others were not. The question was, why? In addition, many organizations that adopted progressive management struggled or failed in their efforts to transform. Some bumbled along for years or decades while others gave up. What was the connection between those outcomes and the organizations' top leaders?

The study of success is complementary to the study of failure. In other words, not doing the things that lead to success can obviously be considered factors that contribute to struggle and failure. Was it that simple? Or was there more to it than that? I was curious and wanted to further my understanding because struggles and failure were so common while success was so rare.

In 2007, I began to shift my focus from Lean transformation success to understanding the causes of failure. This was a time when the struggles and failures experienced by people and organizations were largely ignored by Lean movement leaders -- both individuals and organizations. Like my study of leadership starting in 1994, the careful study of struggles and failures were fresh grounds to explore. I was excited about that and tirelessly pursued answers to the many questions I had.

At the same time, I was perplexed as to why the leaders of the Lean movement, people we respected and admired, had largely ignored this important problem for decades. They continued along the path established in the 1980s of recognizing and promoting only the success stories. I thought this was irrational. Failures exist; they are real and must be studied so that others do not make the same mistakes. Furthermore, to ignore struggles and failures is to be fundamentally inconsistent in relation to the "Respect for People" principle – also seemingly irrational. As an engineer, I am interested in both why something works and why something fails. We do not ignore bridge or aircraft that fail. We should not ignore Lean transformation process struggles and failures. People are harmed in either case, which gives ample justification for studying the latter.

As I began this new line of study, I was certain many others would be as interested in it as I was. After all, so much time, effort, and money were put into transforming organizations that people would surely want to know why they failed and what they could do to improve. I worked on this problem for more than 10 years, assuming a ready audience for this new knowledge. But, year after year, I was confronted by indifference or hostility, particularly in my imperfect communication of findings via social media. Criticism was invariably about tone but not the substance of my work. That suggested a great sensitivity to the forceful exposing of truths that might undercut the relevancy or stated effectiveness of Lean management.

Getting to the truth is what an engineer does. It is also what one learns in kaizen – that we should expose the truth, see reality as it is, and then improve the process (or self) without blame or judgment. But, can truths about Lean management be exposed and gain the same level of interest as truths on the shop or office floor that signal the need for process improvement? My experience says no. *Irrational Institutions* explores this and other phenomena.

During the earlier period when I focused on Lean success [1], my work was accepted and lauded by many. I was in demand as a conference speaker and executive trainer. My subsequent focus on Lean transformation struggles and failure made me a marginalized man – marginalized from mainstream Lean thinking and practice and marginalized from Lean community leaders. They and others characterized me as overly assertive, intellectually arrogant, self-promoting, and possessing a negative attitude. Some people spoke ill of me to render my work irrelevant. My work was seen as inflammatory and irritating, and alienated many powerful or influential people. Demand for my work faded away. This is the downside of intellectual iconoclasm. I accept the blame and consequences, and I understand how my work exposed the pathological traits and structural impediments that exist in the Lean community.

My work also exposed the hypocrisy of the apostles of problem-solving, which is to work only on those problems that the community of leading Lean thinkers deem acceptable. The avoidance of causal explanations for Lean struggles and failures and the emulatory nature of Lean promotion both struck me as irrational. And, conversely, my work was seen by others to be irrational. People were perplexed at how I could be both an enthusiastic supporter of Lean management and a harsh critic. Doesn't one undo the other? No, what it does is it paints a full picture of both the opportunities and difficulties, rather than only half of the picture. This brings us to the present work.

Marginalization has an upside: the ability to see from the outside in. This vantage point offers the freedom to do things that cannot be done from the inside. Besides, I do not share the preconceptions, values, or pecuniary drive that animates many of my colleagues inside the Lean movement. This is not a statement of superiority; it is merely who I am.

Estrangement from the Lean milieu helps me do what I do, which is to provide an outside view that the Lean movement can use to improve, or not. Some people appreciate that, others do not.

Many Lean movement leaders and top influencers cite the work of Dr. W. Edwards Deming as their guiding light. His words have proved prophetic in relation to the advancement of Lean management [2]:

> "A system cannot understand itself. Understanding comes from outside. An outside view provides a lens for examination of our present actions, policies... Far better, more trustworthy, is an outside view, a new way of looking at things. It is only by that outside view that we get ahead."

The "system," in this case, is the leading people and organizations who promote Lean management. It is a system of habits, relationships, and methods that has long been internally focused and, as I have learned first-hand, resistant to outside views. Thus, Lean management struggles to gain wider acceptance among business and other leaders. Doing more in the future of what was done in the past to promote Lean is unlikely to yield the desired results.

Irrational Institutions builds upon an earlier work, *The Triumph of Classical Management Over Lean Management: How Tradition Prevails and What to Do About It* [3], which critically examined the institution of leadership and provided a comprehensive explanation for why leaders resist or reject Lean management. *The Triumph of Classical Management* identified a massive countervailing force to Dr. Deming's "System of Profound Knowledge" (SoPK) designed to enable progress [4] – a force that is both very efficient and astonishingly effective at obstructing progress: the "System of Profound Privilege" (SoPP). The two systems, shown in Figure P-1, are highly antagonistic and work against one another, SoPP being far stronger than SoPK, resulting in the status quo. This outside view has met with praise from Lean practitioners and disinterest from Lean movement leaders and top Lean influencers.

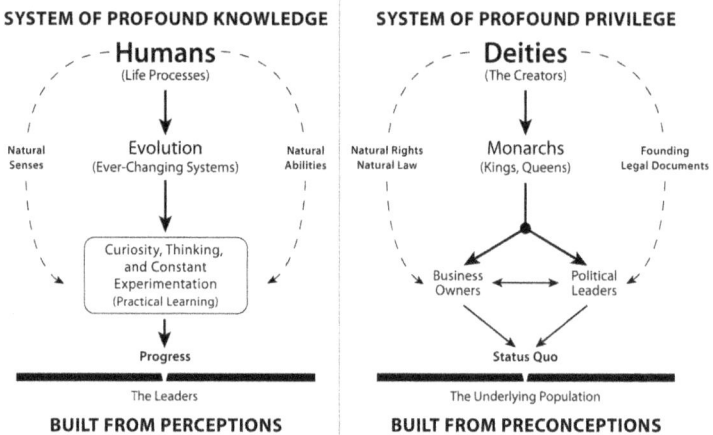

SYSTEM OF PROFOUND KNOWLEDGE   SYSTEM OF PROFOUND PRIVILEGE

Humans   **Deities**
(Life Processes)   (The Creators)

Natural   Evolution   Natural   Natural Rights   Monarchs   Founding
Senses   (Ever-Changing Systems) Abilities Natural Law   (Kings, Queens) Legal Documents

Curiosity, Thinking,   Business   Political
and Constant   Owners   Leaders
Experimentation
(Practical Learning)

Progress   Status Quo

The Leaders   The Underlying Population

BUILT FROM PERCEPTIONS   **BUILT FROM PRECONCEPTIONS**

Figure P-1. In SoPK, humans are at the forefront and leaders are enablers of progress. In SoPP, leaders are at the forefront while the underlying population serves a functional role. In SoPK, select people pass through the small hole at the bottom to lead the progress of humanity. In SoPP, leaders draw select people up from the underlying population to support their business or political interests and to help maintain the status quo.

It is important to continue this work and examine the problem from different directions, as shown in Figure P-2. It may prove fruitful to examine the problem from additional directions as this could lead to other solutions.

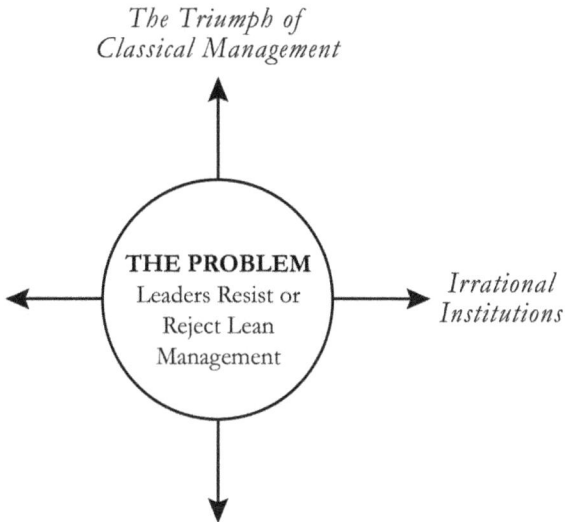

The Triumph of
Classical Management

THE PROBLEM
Leaders Resist or
Reject Lean
Management

Irrational
Institutions

Figure P-2. Analysis of the problem from different directions.

Irrational Institutions seeks to answer the same question, why leaders resist or reject Lean management, but in a different way. Why bother doing this? Because the problem of advancing progressive management becomes more pressing as time goes by. Classical management, rooted in the ancient past, is no longer useful in a time of rapid change marked by digitization of work and life, social disruption, income stagnation, political instability, authoritarian leadership, corporate oligopoly and monopoly, irrelevance of facts, changing work skills, reversals in global trade, climate change, and many other forces. Progressive management will not gain broader acceptance if all one does is promote the rare success stories. The causes of Lean transformation process failure are a complex interconnected network that must be carefully studied from different directions.

Compared to *The Triumph of Classical Management*, *Irrational Institutions* is less about leaders and more about the common social habits of thought and action that lead to observable outcomes. It examines how irrationality is designed into the institutions of business, leadership, and the Lean movement, thus assuring that progressive management will likely remain a niche practice for the foreseeable future, assuming it even survives as it is currently understood. It describes how irrationality is inseparable from human thought and action, and how efforts to impose rationality are often destined to fail. *Irrational Institutions* also critiques the aesthetics of the institution of leadership and the Lean movement, and describes how their aesthetics function as powerful mechanisms to maintain the status quo despite the obvious need for change.

This new mode of critical analysis stands on its own in answering the question of why most leaders prefer classical management and remain committed to it, despite the existence of more rational choices of management practice. *Irrational Institutions* complements the findings of *The Triumph of Classical Management*, but it analyzes the problem in ways that might be judged by some as less offensive or more benign, and illuminates pathways for gaining wider acceptance of Lean management.

Curiosity has always been a motivating force for me. Simply put, all I have wanted to do is understand what is going on; why things succeed or fail. Perhaps you want to understand this as well. The benefit is more knowledge which leads to a better understanding of problems, better problem-solving, and better decision-making. It also leads to a calmness in finally knowing what is actually going on.

Bob Emiliani
South Kingstown, Rhode Island
January 2020

Notes

[1] Success in Lean transformation can be defined as achieving a transformation from classical (traditional) management thinking and practices, characterized by adversarial relationships and batch-and-queue material and information processing, to Lean management characterized by cooperative relationships and a continuous or near-continuous flow of material and information. The transformation, which includes substantial changes in leadership thinking and activities, results in the creation of a "Lean culture" where all employees engage in daily problem-solving using various structured methods and tools to improve processes (i.e. the application of scientific thinking to eliminate waste, unevenness, and unreasonableness). Simply put, the organization becomes Toyota-like in its thinking and practices, using the scientific method and its derivatives (kaizen, PDSA, A3 reports) for the purpose of serving customers, to be flexible and adaptable to changing conditions (in markets, technology, the workplace, society, and the environment), and to help assure long-term survival.

References

[1] Emiliani, B. *et al.* (2007), *Better Thinking, Better Results: Case Study and Analysis of an Enterprise-Wide Lean Transformation*, second edition, The CLBM, LLC, Wethersfield, Conn.

[2] Stevens, T. (1994), "Dr. Deming: 'Management Today Does Not Know What Its Job Is' (Part 2)," *Industry Week*, 18 January, https://www.industryweek.com/operations/quality/article/21963886/dr-deming-management-today-does-not-know-what-its-job-is-part-2, accessed 14 December 2019

[3] Emiliani, B. (2018), *The Triumph of Classical Management Over Lean Management: How Tradition Prevails and What to Do About It*, Cubic, LLC, South Kingstown, Rhode Island

[4] Deming, W. (1994), *The New Economics: For Industry, Government, Education*, Second Edition, Chapter 4, The W. Edwards Deming Institute, Ketchum, Idaho

Introduction

The title of this book is *Irrational Institutions*. What does it mean? Let's look at each word separately, beginning with irrationality. What is irrationality? What does it mean to be irrational? These terms are generally understood to mean that a *person* is not logical in their thinking and actions; that they are unreasonable. In this book, irrationality is not focused on the person, but on the preconceptions used by people to order and formulate their thinking and guide their actions. The focus is the *thing* that is irrational, such as a preconception. What is a preconception? It is a preconceived idea or prejudice; an untested assumption. An assumption can sometimes exist as a belief that may or may not be testable, the latter being a type of superstition. Often, preconceptions are irrational because they are untested but assumed to be true and reliable for the purposes of thinking and decision-making. Cognitive biases generate distortions in perceptions that confirm preconceptions and invariably manifest as irrationality that blocks progress.

What is an institution? It is commonly understood to be a formal organization consisting of people in a hierarchy who perform various coordinated activities to fulfill its goals and purpose. "Institution" can also refer to a collection of organizations within a specified group. Examples include government, non-governmental organizations, non-profit organizations, healthcare, professional societies, banking, industry, retail trade, higher education, military, law enforcement, ecclesiastical organizations, business, and so on. This is not the meaning of "institutions" that is used in this book. Rather, "institution" means *social habits of thought and action*, particularly in relation to the common view of what a problem is and how problems should be solved. These habits coalesce to make individual and group behavior predictable, and include explicit or implicit rules, customs, routines, traditions, as well as spiritual or mystical beliefs. These habits establish a social context and processes that may either serve to protect or disrupt the status quo. The social habits of thought and action are often seen as unique to an individual organization or group of organizations. People who move between different fields, say from healthcare to higher education, learn that the social habits of thought and action may not be as unique as is thought by those who instead remain within a field such as healthcare throughout their career.

The title, *Irrational Institutions*, therefore, means *the social habits of thought and action that are irrational*, common to individuals in a social group. These exist alongside social habits of thought and action that are rational. Trouble comes to organizations when the social habits of thought and action are mostly irrational. This occurs when preconceptions are irrational and cannot be corrected by the social habits of thought and action that are rational.

The word "irrational" requires further elaboration and analysis because it is a core concept in this book, and it is of critical importance in answering the question of why most leaders prefer classical management over Lean management. From that can come possible solutions to this and other problems related to maintaining the status quo.

We make use of our unique ability as humans to reason. That means we use logic to order our thoughts and actions and to harmonize our lived experiences. Our logic can be bad or good. If our logic is judged by self or others to be good, it referred to as "sound." If our logic is judged by self or others to be bad, we say it is "irrational." Whether sound or irrational logic prevails, there is an unending flow of problem creation and problem-solving. Rationality and irrationality are a type of *yin* and *yang* in human experience. The dark side, *yin*, is irrationality while the bright side, *yang*, is rationality. Together the two travel with humans through their lived experiences over time. Rationality and irrationality are inseparable from human existence.

Because irrationality is judged to be bad in human thought and action, efforts are made to eradicate it and replace it with reason. But is that even possible? If we try too hard to be rational, is that not likely to generate irrationality? Does irrationality serve a useful function such that eradicating it might cause more problems than it solves? What if certain types of social organizations have irrationality built-in to their fundamental workings under the tested or untested assumption that it helps ensure prosperity or survival? And what do we mean by survival? Is it short- or long-term; years, decades, or centuries? What if irrationality cannot be eliminated? Is it possible to live more comfortably with it?

What if, through certain habits of thought and action, a social organization is successful in having reason prevail for some extended period of time? Can it withstand the introduction of habits of thought and action that are the opposite – an infusion of irrationality, which to some, perhaps many, might feel like a welcome change from the rigors of daily reason. Thinking of rationality and irrationality as a *yin* and *yang* of human experience establishes a more realistic understanding and expectation of human thought and action. Rationality has the potential to produce irrationality, just as irrationality has the potential to produce rationality. Reason and unreason should be thought of as two sides of a coin, with humans alternating between them as we seek to find a harmonious balance in our existence day-to-day and year-to-year.

Organizations, and businesses in particular, typically have as their mission to produce goods and services that customers desire. People and processes are arranged in different ways to achieve the desired outcomes. The arrangements can be more favorable to the organizations' interests or more favorable to the customers' interests. The arrangement of people and processes will be the result of a combination of rational and irrational thought (i.e. design) and result in a combination of rational and irrational action. Productive activities can be arranged in ways that are mostly irrational and require the sustained use force to obtain the result. Alternatively, productive activities can be arranged in ways that are mostly rational and require the lighter hand of persuasion to obtain the result.

The preceding paragraph broadly described the common and uncommon ways people and processes are arranged to achieve desired outcomes: batch-and-queue material and information processing, characteristically found in classical management, and flow processing of material and information, characteristically found in Lean management. If a person were unaware of flow processing, batch-and-queue material and information processing would seem entirely rational; a product of logical thinking, though people would constantly complain that many things are difficult to do. But the arrangement, the system, would be accepted by all, from CEO to worker, because they know of no other way to produce goods and services that customers desire. And they might not have any logical basis to seek a better arrangement of people and processes because the system they created works.

If a person were aware of flow processing, then batch-and-queue material and information processing would seem entirely irrational; a product of illogical thinking, and they would understand why people constantly complain that the work is difficult to do. The scientific thinking (i.e. application of the scientific method) that is required to produce material and information flow, which is based on perceptions, suggests it is a more rational way to produce goods and services that customers desire. But wait! Wasn't scientific thinking used to create batch-and-queue material and information processing? Generally, no, though some specific aspects may have utilized scientific thinking.

Conversely, if a person familiar with batch-and-queue processing were to see flow processing, established modes of illogical thinking and preconceptions would make them see flow processing as irrational and reinforce their view that batch-and-queue processing is both logical and right. If each person is challenged to convince the other of the merits of their system, conflict erupts that pitches preconceptions (batch-and-queue) against perceptions (flow), and illogical and logical reasoning are defended using arguments that may or may not be sound given that there are no ground rules for argumentation. In other words, the owners of each reality (batch-and-queue and flow) are correct given the information that each possesses.

This helps us understand why a continued focus on Lean success stories is unlikely to produce anything more in the future than it has in the past. A quasi-equilibrium situation has emerged between systems whose arrangement is based on preconceptions (classical management) and systems whose arrangement is based on perceptions (Lean management), supported by whatever combination of logical and illogical thinking may be needed as conditions change over time. Forcefully pushing reason – the scientific thinking that produces material and flow – will soon give way to unreason among those who cherish reason.

Batch-and-queue material and information processing exists because of so-called "lazy thinking." It features illogical modes of thinking such as [1]:

- Expediency – Ignoring the means to achieve the desired ends; doing what is most convenient.
- Using and Abusing Tradition – "It's always been done this way."
- Abuse of Expertise – "Just do as I say."

These three forms of illogical thinking, at their root, ignore evidence that could be used to formulate a counterargument that batch-and-queue material and information processing is a poor way to produce goods and services that customers desire. In addition, batch-and-queue material and information processing is based on numerous preconceptions, not perceptions, which suggest that it is the preferred way to arrange people and processes. These preconceptions include:

- Economies of scale
- More efficient to produce in batches
- Cheaper to buy in bulk
- Must obtain the lowest unit costs
- Need leverage to get results
- Inventories are an asset
- Must force people to do things

Lazy thinking is not meritless. It can indeed create workable arrangements of people and processes that successfully produce goods and services that customers desire. Lazy thinking produces something else that can be seen as very useful: power – especially political power. The results of lazy thinking can thus be adequate to the need.

Yet, rigorous (logical) thinking can produce arrangements that are better for the producer, customer, and other stakeholders. However, no organization has perfect material and information flow in all processes, and flow processing is never perfect. There always exists a combination of flow and batch-and-queue processing, the rational and irrational, which are in constant flux and which impinge one another. And because of perpetually changing conditions, one or the other, rationality or irrationality (which embodies feelings and sentiments), sets off irrationality or rationality in people and processes. So, there is never one right, logical answer for all time that can permanently displace an illogical answer. Humans do not, and cannot, function under logic as the one supreme authority.

Instead, there is a never-ending tension between the dark side, *yin*, irrationality, and the bright side, *yang*, rationality. Just as a day that is all bright or all dark is unsuitable for humans over the long-term, an existence that is entirely rational or entirely irrational is likewise unsuitable for humans over the long-term. Both mental faculties are needed for sense-making and survival. Importantly, irrationality is independent of intelligence. People can be both irrational and intelligent, whether they are CEO or shop floor worker [2, 3].

It is possible to be overly reverent to logic as that which unfailingly reveals the truth. This, itself, is an error in thinking caused by unreason. Reason can easily be corrupted by sentiments, self-interest, or traditions. For example, even though logical thinking can produce arrangements that are better for the producer, customer, and other stakeholders, efforts to push flow onto others will soon, if not automatically, become corrupted by self-interest. A seemingly rational choice, self-interest, leads to irrational thinking and actions. This opens fruitful avenues for criticism by those who are convinced of the validity of their preconceptions and who may honestly question the link between rationality and progress.

These introductory pages provide initial insights into why most leaders prefer classical management and remain committed to it, despite the existence of more rational choices of management practice. It reveals a complex situation that should not be unexpected or surprising given the disappointing results that have been observed with respect to Lean transformation. Subsequent pages examine irrationality found in the institutions of business and leadership, and the Lean movement. Specifically, the social habits of thought and action that are irrational. From this construction we will examine the aesthetics of the institution of leadership and the Lean movement to further our understanding of how aesthetics help maintain the status quo. This begs the question of what to do about it if one wants to make progress towards better work and life.

There are natural phenomena that could be curative. For example, irrationality that supports the status quo is not destiny. It could unexpectedly collapse under its own weight and lead to a different ratio of rationality-to-irrationality. Or, circumstances can suddenly change to produce a "new reality" that replaces the current rationality-irrationality. Self-interest plays a principal role in business, leadership, and the Lean movement. Therefore, it should not be surprising that things may change when the need to do so is felt in relation to the preconception of self-interest. The change that occurs may or may not be better. The following chapters will explore these possibilities.

Questions to Reflect On

- A preconception shared by economists and top business leaders is that markets ensure efficient outcomes regardless of the management system used. Are they right? If so, can you prove it?

- Irrational thinking can be a major force in extinguishing a business and people's livelihoods (and lives, through depression, despondency, suicide). Most organizations and nearly all people have a strong desire to avoid being harmed, avoid doing harm to others, and survive. What types of rational thinking can help people and business avoid harm and survive (see References 2 and 3)?

- Irrational thinking is easy to see in others but difficult to see in one's self. Can you generate a list of irrational thinking that you have witnessed by your leaders? Categorize the list and try using it to help you develop a better ratio of rational-to-irrational thinking.

- What can you do to avoid lazy thinking? How can you help others avoid lazy thinking?

References

[1] McInerny, D. (2005), *Being Logical: A Guide to Good Thinking*, Random House, New York, New York

[2] Stanovich, K. (2016), "The Comprehensive Assessment of Rational Thinking," *Educational Psychologist*, Vol. 51, No. 1, pages 23-34. http://www.keithstanovich.com/Site/Research_on_Reasoning_files/Stanovich_EdPsy_2016.pdf

[3] Erceg, N., Galić, Z., and Bubićb, A. (2019), "'Dysrationalia' Among University Students: The Role of Cognitive Abilities, Different Aspects of Rational Thought and Self-Control in Explaining Epistemically Suspect Beliefs," *European Journal of Psychology*, Vol. 15, No. 1, pages 159–175. https://www.ncbi.nlm.nih.gov/pmc/articles/PMC6396694/

1

The Institution of
of Business

ir·ra·tion·al *adj* 1. Not logical or reasonable

in·sti·tu·tion *n* 1. Social habits of thought and action

"What's next is most likely to be determined by what is."

- Douglas F. Dowd

The Institution of Business

Business seems to be such a normal activity given our daily interaction with it as employees, customers, suppliers, or investors. Our experiences surely vary, but on balance they are mostly positive. Yet, business is actually a peculiar, otherworldly activity because its basic function rests on irrational assumptions about humans and how they interact and transact with one another in an economy.

Seventeenth- and eighteenth-century Enlightenment philosophers, seeking to distance man from the feudal past and the then monarchical present, proffered a view of humanity as individuals free to do as they please, liberated from restrictions imposed by the state or social norms. This formed the foundation for classical and neoclassical economics and the creation of *Homo economicus*, economic man, a man-made (not God-made) fictional actor self-interested in the pursuit of ends that they seek, under the assumption that society always and forever benefits. Previously, the motive for one's work was service and self-sacrifice to fellow human beings and the community.

As with any new idea there can be much good that comes from it. But there can also be consequences that were not anticipated, leading to outcomes that were neither sought nor desired. While simplification of existential phenomena for the purpose of detailed analytical study is a valid scientific technique and often results in needed progress that is beneficial to humanity, it can have limits beyond which it falters.

The reduction or re-construction of *Homo sapiens* ("wise man" in Latin), a social animal acting in group interests, into free-willed individuals acting in their own self-interest, *Homo economicus*, is a substantial change in perspective, even if limited to economic transactions – but recognizing that this category of transactions constitutes a large portion of human activity. Free-willed individuals acting in their own self-interest was termed "rational," while human's acting in the interests of their social group was termed "irrational." The term "rational" may have been selected to help gain acceptance for this radically new idea. After all, the phrase "irrational self-interested maximizer" does not sound like something you or I would like to be characterized as. Instead, we like to think of ourselves as "rational" and will admit only occasionally to being "irrational." We believe we are far more logical than illogical in the execution of our individual and collective life processes.

Characterizing free-willed individuals acting in their own self-interest as "rational" is an imaginary truth, not an actual truth, that offers an easy justification for myriad forms of irrational behavior in the conduct of economic activity. It is apparent on its face that higher-order thinking is required for decision-making in social groups than decision-making that narrowly considers one's self-interest. If we think principally in terms of individual self-interest, whether "individual" means a person or a corporation, we quickly become lazy thinkers and are more likely to do harm to others – assuming one is even cognizant of that possibility, given that the word "rational" suggests such an outcome is not possible. Through lazy thinking we create a world in which zero-sum outcomes become more common that non-zero-sum outcomes. Then, sometime later, we wonder why people are unhappy, why they are difficult to engage, why they feel left out, or why they become subversive.

"Rational" means logical thinking; that reason is the guiding force in thinking and actions in economic activity. That suggests logical thinking by both managers and workers in the conduct of business. But upon close inspection, one finds two different modes of thinking in a corporation: *de jure* (by right) for leaders, and *de facto* (by fact) for workers [1]. These modes of thinking produce different ratios of rationality-to-irrationality depending upon the nature of one's work. Workers must deal with the facts of a situation in order to produce a product or service according to the designer's specifications and to satisfy customer demand. Workers, therefore, must be high in rationality and low in irrationality. Leaders, not engaged in the same facts as workers, and possessing the ability to make decisions by whim or by fact, tend to be higher in irrationality than rationality.

For example, zero-sum outcomes are common in the conduct of business. Decisions made by leaders that are good for the company are often bad for employees, customers, suppliers, and sometimes even investors. Yet, such outcomes are termed "rational" from the perspective of the classical economics by which corporations operate and by which most leaders think and act. So, it can be confusing that leaders higher in irrationality than rationality, would understand themselves to be higher in rationality than irrationality. In other words, leaders understand their decisions to be sound and therefore void of lazy thinking. But, often, that is not the actual case. Many decisions are unsound and caused by lazy thinking. Lower-level people who point this out to leaders are marginalized because it undermines leaders' social habits of thought and action. It challenges their institution. Where workers may see persistent dysfunctionality and stasis, leaders may see a good arrangement of people and processes making steady progress toward perfection. Who is right?

Thus, the corporation – the corporate body as animated by its leaders – in the conduct of business, is not devoted to scientific thinking as a regular feature throughout the hierarchy. Scientific thinking being the curiosity that motivates people to study and learn for its own sake or to solve practical problems related to the production of goods and services. Instead of facts on the ground, leaders' thinking and action is based on metaphysical indicators of performance such as financial statements, performance metrics, spreadsheets, and the opinion of peers or direct reports. There is also a dependence on other metaphysical qualities such as salesmanship, boosterism, and, in some cases, hucksterism. An example of this is adherence to a plan despite facts that prove the plan is no longer valid, useful, or attainable.

Accepting the "rational self-interested maximizer" construct means that business will be guided partly, if not mostly, by irrationality (e.g. zero-sum outcomes among social groups). This introduces a structural defect that orients itself towards the status quo and makes business resistant to improvement (correction of defects) because facts are not uniformly recognized throughout the hierarchy. Yet we know that business cannot exist on rational thinking alone. Some irrational thinking is needed for sense-making and survival, regardless of one's position in the hierarchy.

Figure 1-1 shows two pie charts depicting ratios of rational and irrational thinking by workers (top chart) and leaders (bottom chart). Workers producing goods and services understand facts as necessary for rational thought and action in relation to productive work and problem-solving. Leaders understand self-interest as necessary for rational thought and action in relation to business results such as sales, profits, and growth. From this we can understand why workers and leaders have difficulty understanding each other; why communication may be perpetually confused and why plans may not be understood or followed. The thinking needed for sense-making and survival in each social group varies depending upon the type of work one does – whether it is fact-based (workers' work based on perceptions of good or bad quality goods or services) or metaphysical (leaders' work based on preconceptions related to corporate purpose and business results).

The pie charts in Figure 1-1 can be understood as depicting, at a high level, the institution of workmanship (top) and the institution of leadership (bottom). The chart for workers is more closely aligned with the historical motive for one's work: service and self-sacrifice to fellow human beings and the community. The chart for leaders is closely aligned with

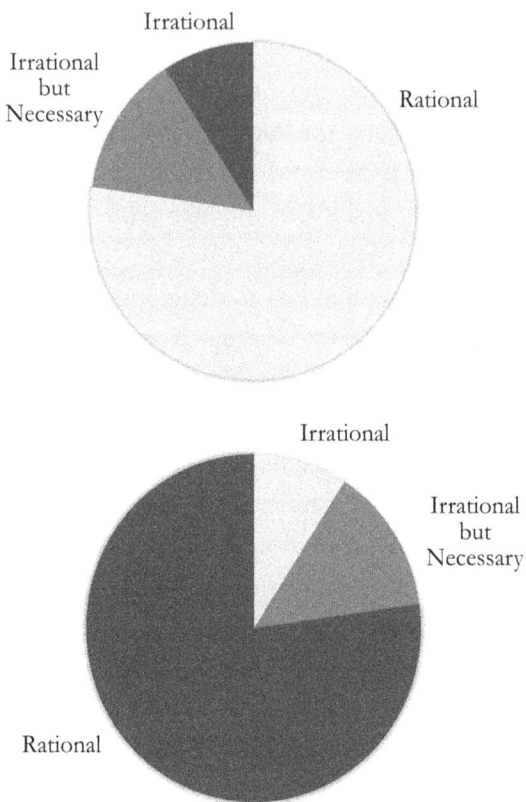

Figure 1-1. Rational-Irrational thinking ratios based on one's
work. Workers (top) and leaders (bottom). Note how
the segment colors and labels are reversed.

the more recent motive for one's work: self-interest in pursuit of the economic ends that they and business seek. While mostly distinct, these two institutions are integrated into institution of business. The three institutions, as well as their integration, are imperfect, though the need for improvement is most often directed towards the institution of workmanship, under the assumption that it is irrational in its aims and hence in perpetual need of fixing by leaders.

If we understand the institution of leadership to represent those most competent in corporate pecuniary interests and the institution of workmanship to represent those most competent in the processes used for the production of goods and services, then we can deepen our understanding of Figure 1-1. Figure 1-2, below, begins with the common assumption that money competence is equivalent to process competence (top). Yet money competence is competence for metaphysical aspects of business based on preconceptions and are not equivalent to facts based on perceptions (middle). Most often, the relationship between money competence and process competence is an inverse relationship (bottom). Self-interest associated with money

$$\text{Money Competence (Irrational)} = \text{Process Competence (Rational)}$$

$$\text{Money Competence (Metaphysical)} = \text{Process Competence (Facts)}$$

$$\text{Money Competence (Metaphysical)} = \frac{1}{\text{Process Competence (Facts)}}$$

Figure 1-2. Assumed (top, middle) and actual relationship (bottom) between money competence and process competence.

competence does not exist in the same way as for process competence, which is driven more by curiosity and quality.

Self-interest in the pursuit of one's ends is obviously something that can be very appealing. Enlightenment philosophers and the classical and neoclassical economists made this even more appealing by arguing that human beings had intrinsic or natural (God-given) rights to life, liberty, and property, including the freedom by owners to do as they wish with their property (inclusive of tangible and intangible property). Added to this was the idea of *laissez-faire* ("let [them] do"), which means private parties can transact among themselves free of state intervention or regulation.

Previously, self-interest in the pursuit of one's ends, natural rights, and freedom to transact were reserved for monarchs. Now, these privileges were in the hands of the common man. These were revolutionary ideas that gained greater and greater acceptance over time. Individual profit-seeking, whether financial or material, was legitimized. What was once considered a unworthy and base motive was now argued to be both an appropriate and honorable motive. And indeed, to a large extent they are because these ideas have together resulted in benefits to mankind. Unfortunately, the opposite side of the coin, disadvantages, including harm to people, are easily ignored or forgotten.

Through the long-ago work of Enlightenment philosophers, classical economists, and neoclassical economists, they delivered the social habits of thought and action to business.

Namely, the primacy of individuals, natural rights, private property, and freedom from government restriction. The institutions of business and leadership are the forms that follow the function of business as described by Enlightenment philosophers and classical and neoclassical economists.

The grounds on which these arguments are made are irrational because:

- Self-interest negates the fundamental social nature of human beings
- Natural rights reinforce the argument that individuals are isolated units
- Private property diminishes the importance of community and the common stock of human knowledge needed for survival
- *Laissez-faire* denies the imperfect nature of humans and assumes transactions will never result in harm to others

Calling these "rational" does not make them so. Yet, as previously stated, we do not, and cannot live in an entirely rational world. We therefore rightly seek benefits that the institution of business offers and hope that the difficulties can somehow be managed effectively. Often, they cannot. The institution of business establishes grounds for opportunism, force, and fraud whether by individuals or the corporation. These are not rare occurrences.

The business press abounds with stories of opportunism, force, and fraud. It begins with a desire to gain a differential advantage in a transaction based on the four points listed previously. The objective is to get a "good deal" which, most often, is a euphemism for winning at someone else's expense. Sustained predation and exploitation may follow. Some examples, driven by self-interest, include:

- Knowingly sell defective goods or services
- Inflate sales or earnings figures
- Bribery
- Price fixing
- Accounting fraud
- Squeezing suppliers for lower prices
- Extracting tax breaks from local authorities in exchange for jobs
- Setting wages in relation to industry peers to justify paying lower wages
- Not financially rewarding workers for increases in productivity
- Job loss and wage stagnation as a result of globalized free trade

These common occurrences are the result of leader's (explicit or implicit) irrational thinking and actions bent on following the money (sales, earnings or stock price). This causes harm to employees, suppliers, investors, and communities. Yet these outcomes are in alignment with the institution of business – the social habits of thought that produce actions that turn out to be favorable or unfavorable (e.g. unethical, illegal) to the interests of business. These patterns of thought and action are long-lasting and transmitted socially from one generation to the next. They are long-lived in part because irrational thinking is transformed into rational thinking for the basis of economic activity, embodying numerous assumptions all of which are taken as true. Inherited social habits, fit for economic interests, are affirmed as rational social behavior – which people fail to see may be at odds with broader community interests.

As powerful as social learning is, there are other factors that maintain the status quo and disrupt efforts to make corrections to the institution of business. Successful leaders stand tall as figures for others to emulate. Emulation is, at its base, rivalry, and rivalry is a sport in which one seeks to outdo another. This often leads to pugnacity and cunning to eclipse rivals' accomplishments. These become habits that generate a rigid mindset with respect to what constitutes success, which, in turn, interfere with adaptive processes that are not allowed to function to their full, effective potential as times change. The locus of improvement becomes force, fraud, and cunning, rather than social habits of thought and action that facilitate adaptive processes such as teamwork and continuous improvement.

The purpose of intelligence is to solve problems that habits fail to solve. The institution of business embodies numerous settled social habits of thought and action that are maladaptive to change. In perpetuating the status quo, they close off avenues of scientific thinking and experiments that would lead to the development of new habits that are adaptive to changes in the business or community environment. When intelligence is not used, the same solutions are applied to common recurring problems, whether in response to rivalry or to achieve better business results [2]. The institution of leadership considers these solutions to be "pragmatic," meaning practical or sensible rather than theoretical. Yet, such solutions are actually better understood as expediency and opportunism ("instrumental rationality"), with the intent to fulfill a self-interested purpose and the hoped-for result of immediate gain or gain in the near future. Contrast this impulse for rapid gratification with having a curiosity to understand the source of the problem and then quickly solving it using scientific thinking. The institution of leadership relies on rote solutions [2] for problem-solving while the institution of workmanship, by the nature of the work, is oriented toward using intelligence in problem-solving – i.e. understanding cause-and-effect.

The institution of workmanship is in constant conflict with the institutions of business and leadership because the latter, being in a superior position, will exert control on the former and seek to repress it. This manifests itself as pressure to "think like the boss" and "be like the boss" (Figure 1-1) not realizing that successfully doing so would come at the expense of the product or service (e.g. solving production and quality problems) – which in turn can diminish business financial and non-financial performance. Middle managers, having one foot in the institution of leadership (*de jure*) and the other foot in the institution of workmanship (*de facto*), commonly face a great struggle to be effective but do not truly understand why.

Despite the shortcomings described, people benefit from the institution of business, the institution of leadership, and the institution of workmanship, and so they are regarded as having value in society and are seen, overall, as being morally sound despite frequent moral or ethical lapses. This being the case, educational systems succeed more in producing employable persons than they do at developing social habits of thought that are rational, critical, and reflective. Said another way, formal education inadequately prepares people for how to cope with continuous change and the need to improve the institutions of business, leadership, and workmanship to keep in step with the times.

An environment imagined as static as the institutions of business and leadership generally see it, when it is in fact dynamic and changing daily, does not build human intelligence at the needed rate. This allows the entry of substitutions for intelligence such as prejudice and discrimination, cognitive biases and psychopathy, class interests, and archaic traditions. These become habits that trump reason and the uptake of better methods. Those who socialize easily become products of the social environment, thus frustrating those who lack such delicate skills for agreement. The only paths available to them are compliance, disagreement, or disobedience. Compliance, being the most common path, preserves the existing social habits of thought and action characteristic of business and leadership, which are seen as stability by some and inertia by others. Compliance is aided by the existence of hierarchy in organizations which define asymmetrical social, political, and economic relationships and legitimizes power relations and resultant zero-sum outcomes. The static hierarchical structure fails to evolve into networks that reflect the dynamic environment and the social nature of human interaction and transactions. While the façade of stability may be helpful for reducing uncertainty, it is an inaccurate representation that reinforces the archaic elements of the institutions of business and leadership, thereby imperiling learning and advancement.

Irrationality excludes the interests of those people and stakeholders who are integral parts of the conduct of business and whose contributions are indispensable, while preconceptions make it effortless to imagine that the costs of institutional adaptation and change to meet evolving human needs vastly exceed the benefits. "What ought to be" is perpetually asphyxiated by "what is." The "what is" remains as-is because it contains many forms of beauty that please leaders' senses. This brings us to the next chapter, which discusses the aesthetics of the institution of leadership in relation to business and classical management.

Questions to Reflect On

- What might business look like if it was based on actual rational assumptions about humans as social beings and how they interact and transact with one another in an economy?

- Referring to Figure 1-1, what can be done to close the gap between the rational-irrational thinking ratios for leaders and workers? In which direction should the gap be closed: towards workers or towards leaders?

- Referring to Figure 1-2, what is it about money competence that subverts a leader's past process competence (when they were a worker)?

- The institution of business is imperfect. What corrections can be made to improve it? Consider both the changes are in your control and those that are not in your control.

- Zero-sum outcomes are a core feature of the institution of business. Considering that no person or organization wants or likes to be the loser, what could be done to produce more balanced outcomes?

References

[1] Emiliani, B. (2018), *The Triumph of Classical Management Over Lean Management: How Tradition Prevails and What to Do About It*, Chapter 3, Cubic, LLC, South Kingstown, Rhode Island

[2] Ibid., Table 1-2: CEOs Wealth Creation Playbook, p. 34

2

The Institution
of Leadership

ir·ra·tion·al *adj* 1. not logical or reasonable

in·sti·tu·tion *n* 1. social habits of thought and action

"Virtually all thoughtful persons… will agree that it
is a despicably inhuman thing for the current
generation willfully to make the way of life
harder for the next generation…"

- Thorstein Veblen

The Institution of Leadership

The previous chapter examined fundamental characteristics of the institution of business. The institution of business is directly connected to the institution of leadership because it is through leaders that the institution of business is actualized in practice. Leaders bring the preconceptions and established social habits of thought and action of economics and business to life. The work done hundreds of years ago by Enlightenment philosophers and economists lives and thrives in today's leaders, evident through sights, sounds, objects, and experiences. Leaders make judgments about these and, given their status and authority, set standards for them. In particular, the institution of leadership sets the aesthetic standards for beauty and ugliness. This is a unique perspective for examining the values of the institution of leadership in relation to the problem under consideration: why leaders resist or reject Lean management. Aesthetics used as an analytical method reveals many new insights.

Aesthetics is a philosophy of beauty, art, and taste. It spans from the creation and appreciation of beauty to the judgment of beauty as experienced by human senses. In the institutions of business and leadership, the sense that is most important is sight, followed by sound. Touch, taste, and smell are of much lesser importance. Situated in between sight and sound and the other senses is intuition, the "gut feeling" that often guides leadership thinking and decision-making. This is an extrasensory perception that best fits the category of spiritual, mystical, or the occult, and becomes a habit of superstition admired by others.

Because the institutions of business and leadership are deeply colored by preconceptions, there is a large domain of sensory perception that judges beauty in relation to the preconceptions. This leads to a timeless and universal understanding of that which is considered beautiful, by sight or sound, and is devoid of cultural conditioning. This also includes judgments of objects and experiences. Therefore, we can say there exists an aesthetic of business and an aesthetic of leadership, and, more broadly, a philosophy of business and a philosophy leadership. The two are so closely integrated that they can seem interchangeable given how Enlightenment philosophy and classical and neoclassical economics thoroughly penetrate both.

Judgment plays a large role in the conduct of business and requires leaders to use sight and sound to discriminate between what is beautiful and what is ugly. Connected to sensory experience is emotional and intellectual activity that aid in making judgments and discerning if something is beautiful. Taste is different in that it is formed through education or socialization processes. It is the result of exposure to objects or experiences that embody variations in values as established by society. For example, society says expensive things are better than inexpensive things, and so expensive wine is judged to be good because it is expensive. The fact that the wine is expensive requires one to be more discerning when drinking it. This, in turn, develops ones' taste (aesthetic) in distinguishing between wine that is good and wine that is bad. This process is heavily influenced by socialization (cultural conditioning), given that only financially successful people can afford to drink expensive wine often enough to be able to develop aesthetic judgments about wine. While taste is embedded in the institutions of business and leadership, the focus in the following pages will be aesthetic judgment because this determines the conduct of business as actualized by the habits of thought and action of leaders.

It can come as no surprise that there is a bias for beauty and a bias against ugliness given the social habits of thought and action and preconceptions. Bias is a substitute for intelligence. In this case, bias for beauty means the cause(s) of ugliness are not of interest. The thing of interest is to praise the beautiful and quickly turn the ugly into the beautiful via expedient means to fulfill a self-interested purpose. The ugly thing, or experiencing difficulty making the ugly thing beautiful, can provoke a physical response caused by the sympathetic nervous system such as accelerated heart rate, elevated blood pressure, pupil dilation, muscle tension, etc., which can emerge as displeasure, hostility, or anger. Conversely, the beautiful can produce physical responses such as a smile, nodding head, or happy tone of voice. We easily observe these in leaders' reactions to what they judge to be beautiful or ugly.

In business, aesthetic judgments of beauty or ugliness are uniform in that they do not vary from one business function to another – for example, from marketing to operations to finance. The aesthetics of business transcends the specific nature of the work performed in each area. Therefore, leaders can move from one company to another or one function to another and quickly distinguish between what is beautiful and what is ugly. They guide human (e.g. workers) behavior based on the universal conceptions of what is beautiful in business activity.

Table 2-1 lists some examples of aesthetic judgments associated with the institution of leadership that are informed by the institution of business. The first category, sight, judges as beautiful the headquarters building and executive office, and the cubicle or factory as ugly. The evidence for this is the absence of any top leader from these areas, often for years at a time, or when headquarters is moved far away from the factory. The peer leader is considered beautiful for two reasons: shared status and

Table 2-1. Examples of Leaders' Aesthetic Judgments

	Beautiful	**Ugly**
Sight	Headquarters	Factory
	Office	Cubicle
	Boss	Worker
	Designer apparel	Budget clothing
Sound	Yes	No
	Okay	But
	Right away	Maybe
	Done!	I can't
	Have the answer	Don't know
Object	Spreadsheets	Product
	Presentation	Report
	Executive summary	Book
Experience	Success	Failure
	Boss	Worker
	Peer	Supplier
	Compliance	Questions
	No problem	Problem
	Meeting	Action item (work)

appearance, where appearance encompasses physical beauty (face, body, hair, skin color, body language) as well as dress. Rarely does one find an ugly senior executive or board member in a large corporation.

The second category, sound, judges as beautiful the words that leaders like to hear and the words they do not like to hear as ugly. The third category, object, judges as beautiful the things that leaders like to interact with and those interactions that they find ugly. The fourth category, experience, judges as beautiful peer interaction and the absence of problems, and interactions with inferiors and problems as ugly.

The aesthetic of institutions is a unique perspective for understanding their stability and the power of the inertia that is encountered by those who wish to affect change. There are many other important aesthetic judgments as they relate to experience. One such judgment is the preference for discrete transactions such as deal-making (beautiful) versus continuous transactions such as those necessary for keeping up with the times (ugly). Strategic business problems are typically solved by deal-making rather than by ongoing change from within, which perpetually lacks the requisite aesthetic in the institution of leadership.

The images on the following pages show common examples of visual aesthetic judgments of beauty and ugliness as defined by the institution of leadership. Readers are challenged to observe and discover additional examples to gain a fuller appreciation of the role of aesthetics in perpetuating the institutions of business and leadership and the practice of classical management.

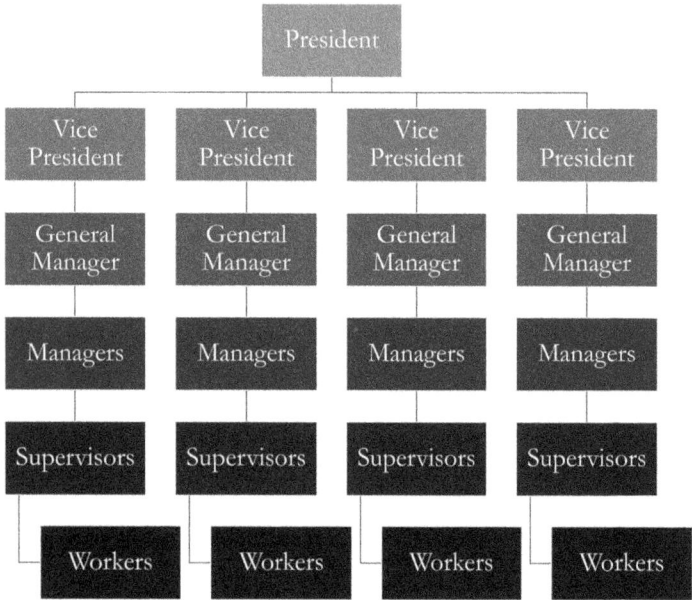

```
                         ┌───────────┐
                         │ President │
                         └───────────┘
   ┌────────────┬────────────┼────────────┬────────────┐
┌──────────┐ ┌──────────┐ ┌──────────┐ ┌──────────┐
│   Vice   │ │   Vice   │ │   Vice   │ │   Vice   │
│President │ │President │ │President │ │President │
└──────────┘ └──────────┘ └──────────┘ └──────────┘
┌──────────┐ ┌──────────┐ ┌──────────┐ ┌──────────┐
│ General  │ │ General  │ │ General  │ │ General  │
│ Manager  │ │ Manager  │ │ Manager  │ │ Manager  │
└──────────┘ └──────────┘ └──────────┘ └──────────┘
┌──────────┐ ┌──────────┐ ┌──────────┐ ┌──────────┐
│ Managers │ │ Managers │ │ Managers │ │ Managers │
└──────────┘ └──────────┘ └──────────┘ └──────────┘
┌──────────┐ ┌──────────┐ ┌──────────┐ ┌──────────┐
│Supervisors│ │Supervisors│ │Supervisors│ │Supervisors│
└──────────┘ └──────────┘ └──────────┘ └──────────┘
  ┌─────────┐ ┌─────────┐ ┌─────────┐ ┌─────────┐
  │ Workers │ │ Workers │ │ Workers │ │ Workers │
  └─────────┘ └─────────┘ └─────────┘ └─────────┘
```

Figure 2-1. Typical corporate organization chart.

The typical visual representation of an organization is a chart depicting the hierarchy of people and their titles. This follows the representation of organizations in feudal times as well as the command and control structure of military organizations. The chain of command passes from top to bottom, and problems at the bottom must pass through each step upward to resolution. The aesthetic associated with this image is beauty because it clearly distinguishes leaders and followers according to rank and maintains the status quo with respect to power, rights, and privileges.

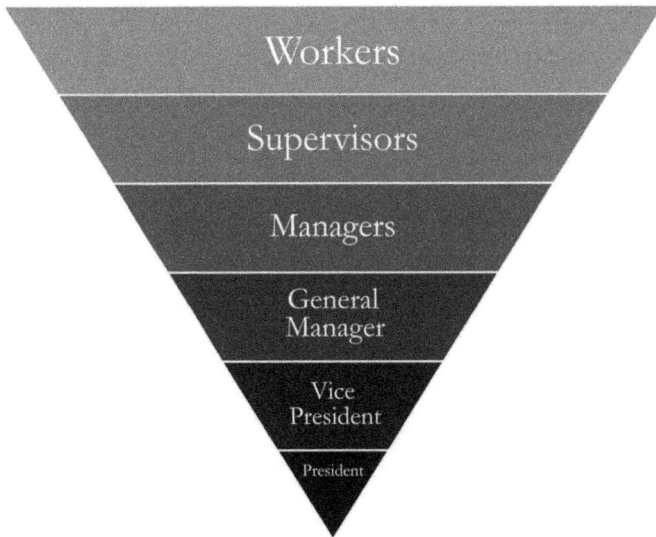

Figure 2-2. Atypical corporate organization chart.

The inverted pyramid is an atypical organization chart whose aesthetic is deemed to be ugly. It contradicts Figure 2-1 where leaders and followers are identifiable by rank, with status and associated respect and honors being clearly identifiable. Figure 2-2 suggests a large loss of status and authority for leaders and a large gain in status and authority for workers. Workers gain status and authority because they are the ones doing the value-added work that customers seek when procuring a product or service. The inverted pyramid is further deemed ugly because it requires changes in thinking, roles, responsibilities, and activities among the leaders, from president to supervisor. It requires leaders to trust and support workers and allow them to think and use their intelligence to help the organization succeed. Workers rely less on instructions from the top and more on independent thinking and decision-making. The inverted pyramid is often associated with the need to achieve greater organizational flexibility and adaptability in response to changing conditions to avoid getting stuck in the status quo. In this chart managers are servant leaders responsible to workers, the opposite that shown in Figure 2-1.

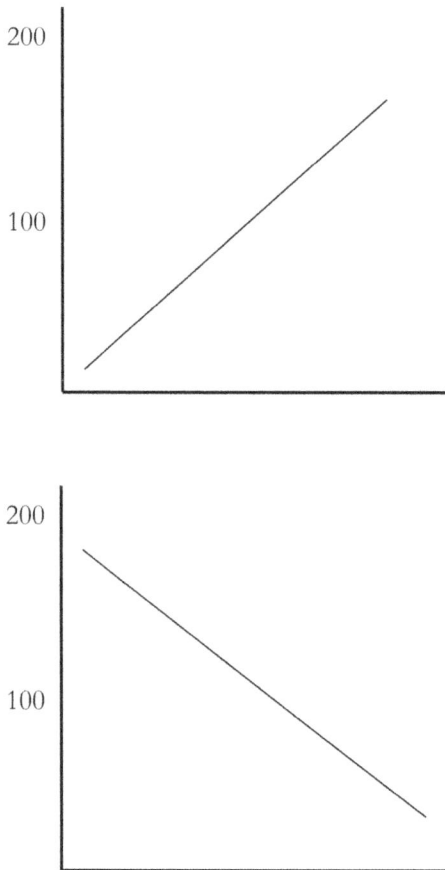

Figure 2-3. Beautiful (top) and ugly (bottom) line charts.

Figure 2-3 (top) shows an aesthetic that is judged to be beautiful and highly valued by the institution of leadership. It shows a leaders' metric or KPI (metaphysical representations of workers' workmanship) that is increasing favorably. The standing requirement for such measures is a steady, uninterrupted increase from one measurement period to the next. This is what leaders like to see and they respond accordingly with favorable physical indicators such as smiling, nodding head, or happy tone of voice. Figure 2-3 (bottom) shows what leaders do not like to see – what is judged to be ugly – and which results in displeasure, hostility, or anger. If, however, the downward trend represents a favorable or improving metric or KPI, then it is judged to be beautiful if steadily decreasing.

People learn the aesthetics of business and leadership early in their work careers through socialization wherein leaders, along with their predecessors, long ago made the aesthetic judgments of beauty and ugliness. Some people eventually become leaders, but few, if any, leaders question these aesthetic judgments and how they might undermine the need for change or impede progress.

Figure 2-4 shows examples of charts normally considered to be ugly. The straight horizontal line (top) is interpretable as no change over time, which generally viewed as ugly given the standard of aesthetic judgment established in Figure 2-3 (top chart). Figure 2-4 (bottom) shows variation in a metric or KPI over time, wherein progress is periodically halted by setbacks. Despite this chart representing real-world conditions, it is judged to be ugly in comparison to the smooth line shown in Figure 2-3 (top). The periodic setbacks occurring in the bottom chart precipitate lengthy explanations to leaders, which may be futile because it reflects common cause (random) variation, but nonetheless lead to the expression of displeasure, hostility, or anger. There can be cases where the charts shown in Figure 2-4 are not judged to be ugly.

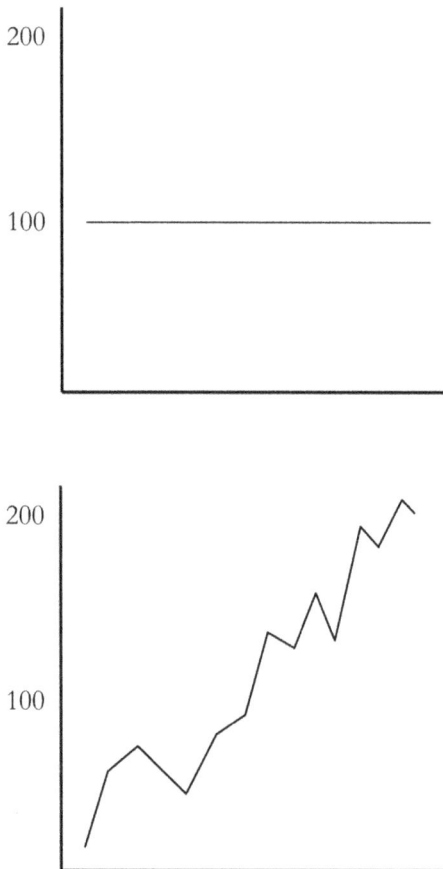

Figure 2-4. Ugly line charts.

Figure 2-5 is another example of a chart that is judged to be ugly due to the large variations in the metric or KPI. If a bar chart looked like Figure 2.3 (top), steadily increasing favorably, then would be judged beautiful.

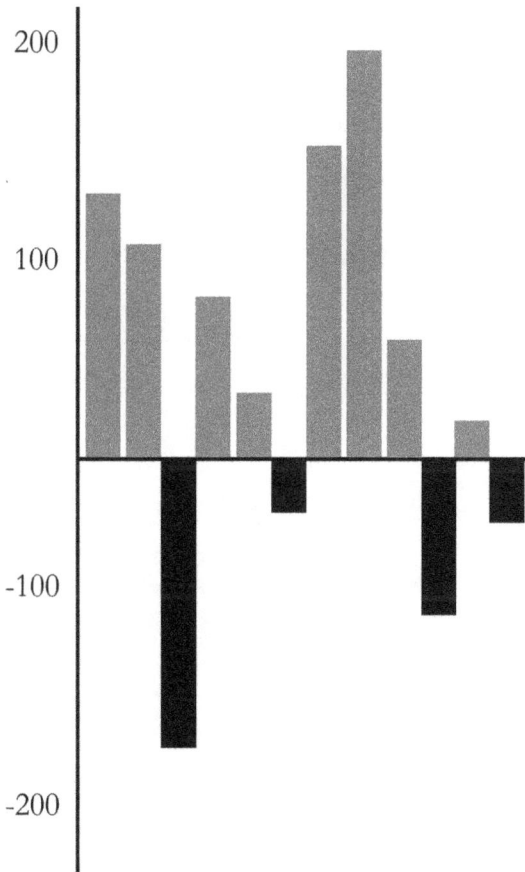

Figure 2-5. An ugly bar chart.

Figure 2-6 shows a beautiful Gantt chart (top) and an ugly Gantt chart (bottom). The top chart is beautiful because all elements of the work breakdown structure are on schedule and, for the sake of illustration, on budget. No work is early or late and no task is under- or over-budget.

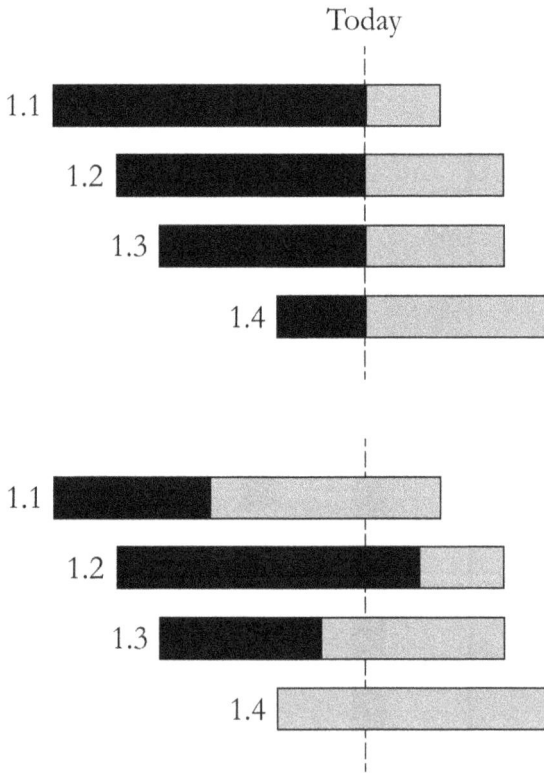

Figure 2-6. Gantt chart, named after the famous early 20th century industrial engineer, Henry Gantt. The top chart is beautiful, the bottom chart is ugly.

The bottom chart is judged to be ugly because no element of the work breakdown structure is on schedule and, for the sake of illustration, no element is on-budget. All work is early or late and tasks are under- or over-budget. Each chart reflects milestones that were either made (top) or missed (bottom) – reflecting success or failure at predicting the future, assuming milestones are not gamed. This precipitates explanations to leaders that lead to the expression of displeasure, hostility, or anger.

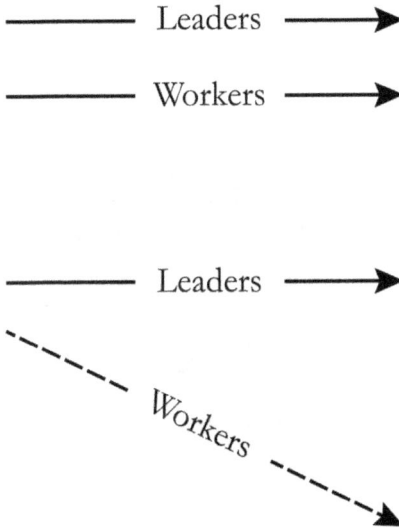

——— Leaders ——→

——— Workers ——→

——— Leaders ——→

Workers

Figure 2-7. Alignment (top) and misalignment (bottom) between leaders and workers.

Workers are expected to be in alignment with the direction set by top leaders. Alignment is judged to be beautiful, as shown in Figure 2-7 (top). Misalignment is ugly (bottom), the result of a gap between leaders' expectations (plan) and the reality of work (actual). Efforts to align workers with leaders often fail, repeatedly, due to the contradictions inherent in classical management. That is, the pecuniary interests of leaders and technical interests of workmanship among workers. Misalignment, therefore, can be persistent and compromise the ability of leaders to meet their commitments to investors and customers. A remedy for misalignment is better and more sustained communication from leaders to workers about strategy, goals, objectives, and plans. Misalignment often continues despite such focused efforts, causing leaders to seek solutions that, combined with other apparent or actual needs, help reduce misalignment.

Figure 2-8. Machine (top) and worker (bottom).

The institutions of business and leadership have a preconception to replace people (ugly) with machines (beautiful) whenever technology allows such changes to be made. This is a routine duty for business leaders. Figure 2-8 illustrates the longstanding, 250-plus year preference for machines over workers. The factors of production in classical economics are labor, land, and capital. Land and capital (financial and capital assets) are owned but labor is not. Because labor is not owned, it is not an asset and therefore does not add to the financial value of a business. Consequently, labor (ugly) is poorly utilized, difficult to align towards management's interests, and troublesome in many other ways (opinions, wages, wage increases, sick days, etc.), and thus is dispensable. Machines (beautiful) are owned assets that increase the value of a business. This includes traditional machines for processing materials, software and hardware for processing information (AI), and electromechanical machines for doing the combined work of material and information processing (robots and automation). Machines are understood by the institution of leadership to unfailingly increase productivity (higher output per unit of resource input) and quality.

Because each organization engaged in business transactions seeks their own self-interested ends, there is little or no incentive to cooperate to achieve shared goals or objectives. Therefore, leaders seek leverage to get things done; to achieve favorable outcomes at someone else's expense. Leverage, of course, is an aesthetic judged as beautiful (Figure 2-9). The more leverage you have over one or more parties, the better. However, repeatedly applying leverage causes other parties to seek to find ways to increase their own leverage as a way to fight back. Soon, the leverage one has is diminished and that gives way to two other things judged to be beautiful: negotiation and deal-making. Negotiation and deal-making are opportunities to win at someone else's expense, thus neutering the opponent's leverage for a time. Failure to win in negotiations is ugly. This unproductive, yet deeply honorific, cycle continues unabated as leaders come and go.

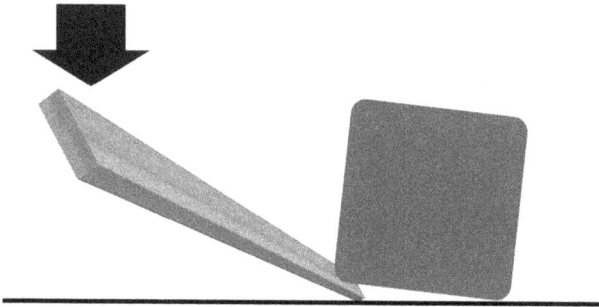

Figure 2-9. Leverage is beautiful.

Figure 2-10 shows our final visual aesthetic judgment of beauty and ugliness as defined by the institution of leadership. The thing of beauty is to receive money from customers or other sources; cash is king. Having to make payments to stakeholders such as local, state, or federal governments is ugly. Likewise, it is ugly to make payments to suppliers. Therefore, it is beautiful to find ways to avoid payment, or to delay or extend payment for as long as possible. This can be done to governments or suppliers because business has leverage, either as part of political processes or intrinsically as with suppliers, especially in cases where the buyer (company) is large and the seller (supplier) is small. It is beautiful to collect money and ugly to dispense money – an exception being dividends paid to shareholders. Money in the form of paychecks must be dispensed to workers on-time and in the correct amounts, and with no disputes. But the dispensing of some monies to workers can be reduced, withheld, or eliminated by eliminating or reducing wage increases or requiring workers to pay more for certain benefits. To do so is beautiful.

Receive Money

Make Payments

Figure 2-10. Money received (top) and money paid (bottom).

Another visual and aural aesthetic judged as beautiful by the institution of leadership is the sight of an audience and the spoken sounds one makes. A large audience of worker's heads nodding in agreement as one speaks, confident of the truth of each word uttered, is beautiful. A lack of enthusiasm, questions, or disagreement among workers is ugly. The phrase "The boss likes to hear himself talk" is commonly uttered in recognition of its beauty within the institution of leadership. In every case, visual or aural ugliness is to be corrected or ignored, and almost never to be considered as a problem to study or useful feedback from which to learn and improve.

There is the intangible aesthetic judgment of "excellence," knowable only to the institution of leadership. The beauty of "excellence" can exist in annual reports yet be absent (or near-absent) within the organization itself. Judgment of "excellence" – hype – embodies the spiritual, mystical, or the occult. Leaders must be adept at these esoteric arts. These aesthetic judgments of beauty and ugliness are easily recognizable to anyone who has worked in organizations, whether large or small. Yet, they likely have not perceived them in the manner presented here and in relation to the problem of leaders resisting or rejecting Lean management.

The timelessness and universality of judgments of beauty assure that an acceptable level of status quo is maintained which, in turn, makes it difficult for the institution of leadership to adapt to changing conditions – despite exhortations made by leaders to workers, commonly perceived by workers as that which leaders desire but are not, in fact, willing to allow happen. For example:

- Be a change agent
- Be a leader and an enabler
- Do the right thing for the company
- Put yourself in your customer's shoes
- Spend company money like it is your own

- Present new ideas and solutions
- Work more efficiently
- Simplify and optimize your work
- Develop talent

The aesthetics valued by leaders suggests an obsession with appearance, and thus the political aspects of organizations and business activity (e.g. cunning, force, fraud). We think of business as an economic organization, but it is better thought of as a political organization whose ends are economic. The façade of the primacy of economic purpose is effective at masking political interests focused on conspicuous beauty. The simplicity of the aesthetics reflects reductionist thinking and narrow self-interest, subject to conspicuous emulation within and between organizations, that imagines idealized, theoretic expressions of beauty as routinely available. This constitutes proof of status, reputability, and leadership.

Business leaders' behaviors have been a subject of great interest in both industry and academia for more than 100 years. It is studied and taught from narrow vantage points, not the broader vantage point as an aesthetic with clearly defined values of beauty and ugliness. An interesting contrast emerges between leaders' view of beautiful leadership behaviors and worker's view of the same – the latter of which is widely characterized as "good leadership" by trainers, leadership coaches, academics, and others. From workers' point of view, beautiful leadership behaviors are non-political in nature, while ugly leadership behaviors are political. In the institution of leadership, beauty and ugliness are reversed, as shown in Table 2-2.

Table 2-2. Aesthetics of Leadership Behaviors

Beautiful Leadership Behaviors as Seen by Leaders	Beautiful Leadership Behaviors as Seen by Workers
Tolerance	Respect
Confidence	Humility
Watchful	Calmness
Erraticism	Consistency
Whim	Deliberation
Telling	Listening
Skepticism	Trust
Personal gain	Sharing
Demanding	Patient
Reactive	Adaptive
Flattery	Sincerity
Bias/Preconception	Intelligence
Calculating	Wisdom
Formal/Ritualistic	Casual/Flexible
Leverage	Cooperation

Despite vast sums of money spent annually to train leaders to behave in ways perceived as beautiful by workers, leaders, overall, continue to behave in ways defined as beautiful by the institution of leadership. As this book and *The Triumph of Classical Management Over Lean Management* show, efforts to improve leadership behaviors is near-futile because it does not address the causes that produce the behaviors, which are embedded in the institution of business and the institution of leadership.

Another less obvious aesthetic that is judged as beautiful is the corporate initiative, often more akin to fads, that is made in response to periodic business problems. All organizations have large problems from time to time that need comprehensive solutions. There are two ways to find such solutions: guess at a solution based on the apparent (surface-level) understanding of the problem or determine the root cause(s) of the problem. The political nature of organizations prevents rigorous root cause analysis because that would expose great deficiencies in leadership, which is ugly to the extreme. Incompetence, ineptitude, bumbling, weakness, embarrassment, humiliation – these appearances are to be avoided at all costs. Therefore, periodic initiatives, expensive fads, and flavors-of-the-month are the go-to curative for organizational ills. Unable to address the root cause(s) of the problem, the initiative trundles along producing some small gains. After a period of time the initiative is declared a success and an expensive new initiative may be initiated. This is an approved method of problem-solving by the institution of leadership.

It should also be noted that something expensive is seen as beautiful if it is authorized by top leaders – such as an initiative, relocation of corporate headquarters, a McKinsey consulting contract, a corporate jet, and so on. From leaders' perspective, labor is expensive, though the money spent is seen as beautiful only when workers are closely aligned with and faithfully execute leaders' directives. Because alignment is rare, the cost of labor is ugly, as are workers' proposals to spend money as if it was not their own. Leaders' displeasure, sometimes hostility, to ugly aesthetics submerges a segment of factual reality that is as much a part of human experience as beauty. As mentioned at the start of Chapter 1, business is a peculiar, otherworldly activity because its basic function rests on irrationality.

A market economy may be confusing and continuously changing, but its aesthetics are crystal clear and stable. The aesthetics of leadership are an idealized or perfected representation of beauty that ignores the messiness and uncertainty found in the actual conduct of business affairs. Consequently, the institution of leadership pressures workers to produce the idealized results (beauty) even though things do not normally work that way. This forces workers to tell the leaders, from supervisor to CEO, what they want to hear and see. This distorts information and results in disruptions, delays, and inaction, thereby sabotaging needed progress. Eventually, it also results in serious corporate distress or failure.

The aesthetics described in this chapter reflect how business functions and for whom it benefits. For example, leading by whim is seen by many as an abuse of power. Or, it is actually a confirmation of power? If so, the aesthetic of whim is beauty, and whim is to be prized, admired, and emulated by other leaders. There is almost nothing in the way of competition for ideas in the institutions of business and leadership. The aesthetics have been worked out and accepted, and they fit squarely within the realm of classical management – largely static and non-evolutionary due to preconceptions and social habits of thought and action. Must times not change to accommodate this?

Questions to Reflect On

- Given the illogical basis of classical and neoclassical economics and the institution of business, do leaders have any choice in having to conform to the institution of leadership and its aesthetics? If so, what are their choices?

- How would you go about redefining the meaning of beauty as seen by leaders to be less distant from beauty as seen by workers?

- The aesthetics of beauty shown in Chapter 2 Figures and Tables powerfully support the status quo. What can be done to weaken or reconfigure these aesthetics of beauty so that progress can be made?

- The institution of leadership, being intimately integrated with the institution of business, will force leaders to make many mistakes. Why don't leaders learn from their mistakes? What can be done to correct that?

- When mistakes are made, blame is invariably assigned to external events, other organizations, or other people. How can one assign mistakes to specific elements of the institution leadership so that corrections can be made?

3

The Lean Movement

ir·ra·tion·al *adj* 1. not logical or reasonable

in·sti·tu·tion *n* 1. social habits of thought and action

"History is strewn with the wreckage left by well-motivated individuals and groups, shattered by forces they did not comprehend and could not control."

- Douglas F. Dowd

The Lean Movement

The previous chapters described how irrationality and the aesthetics associated with the institution of leadership produce a management practice that is disconnected, to greater or lesser extents, from reality; i.e. factual existence. It produces a theoretic of leadership and management that, while workable, causes much more difficulty than is necessary. People who look to improve the practices of leadership and management notice these deficiencies and seek ameliorative solutions. Their improvements are always in the direction towards perception and away from preconceptions. And it includes mindsets and methods that result in the continuous revision of ones' social habits of thought and action. In other words, ameliorative solutions are directed towards creating more rational institutions.

The first major attempt to make more rational institutions of business and leadership was early 20th century Scientific Management. It sought "to prove that the best management is a true science, resting upon clearly defined laws, rules, and principles, as a foundation" [1]. Scientific Management embodied new ways of thinking and new methods of analyzing and improving work that are rooted in perception. It also recognized the social nature of business and sought to improve social and economic relations between management and workers and, "whenever these principles are correctly applied, results must follow which are truly astounding" [1]. The results were indeed "truly astounding" in the establishments that had the full cooperation and personal engagement of top company leaders.

Scientific Management was described this way [2]:

"It is no single element, but rather this whole combination, that constitutes scientific management, which may be summarized as:

- Science, not rule of thumb.
- Harmony, not discord.
- Cooperation, not individualism.
- Maximum output, in place of restricted output.
- The development of each man to his greatest efficiency and prosperity."

The difficulty Frederick Winslow Taylor and others encountered was that few leaders were interested in the complete system of Scientific Management. Instead, they were interested in certain parts of it; the parts that affected workers, to improve productivity and reduce costs. Leaders were uninterested in learning or doing new things that were necessary to support the full "installation" of the Scientific Management system. In 1964, Professor Samuel Haber said the following about the preference among business leaders for only limited adjustments to their existing leadership and management practice [3]:

"The very notion of a completely integrated, scientific system for the factory was a distraction [to businessmen]. The truly 'scientific' standard for 'an honest day's work'... could not be established and maintained unless the entire factory was systematized. Yet most business firms, as Taylor himself once noted, need only be more efficient than their competitors. This was one of the reasons that businessmen preferred efficiency stunts, devices, and mechanisms to a complete system of scientific management. The adoption of a complete system was often not the most profitable use of investment capital. Here... commercial efficiency did not automatically come first. The system should be adopted, Taylor's most orthodox disciples asserted, even when it might not be a paying investment."

In other words, from leaders' perspective, winning by an inch is as good as winning by a mile. Likely even better because, in their view, it costs much less to win in the marketplace by an inch – where costs should be understood to be personal (social and political), as well as financial.

It is clear from the experiences of the Scientific Management movement that business leaders did not want a more rational institution to guide them towards greater business success. They were satisfied with their way of thinking and the existing institution of leadership, and felt that the only changes necessary were that which affected workers engaged in the work of production and low-level administrative work. The ascent of Scientific Management in the early 1900s and its decline by the late 1930s offers wonderful lessons on why leaders resisted or rejected to efforts by people, externally or internally, to impose reason and new habits of thought and action. This, despite the wholesome intention to transition away from zero-sum outcomes and produce better results for all stakeholders. Once again, the political nature of organizations reveals itself and its preference for the status quo – especially among leaders at the top of organizations.

The lessons learned from Scientific Management were largely ignored by those who in subsequent years would seek to advance new management systems and methods rooted in perception. The thinking for that seems to be:

1. Indifference to the past struggles.
2. Assuming that failure was the fault of those who proffered new management systems and methods.
3. Overconfidence in one's ability to substantively change the institutions of business and leadership.
4. Underestimating the strength of traditions [4].
5. Assuming the latest systems or methods for imposing reason and new habits of thought and action will magically succeed where earlier ones failed (irrational belief in superstition).
6. Thinking that stronger and better crafted rational arguments for adopting new systems or methods will be more convincing to leaders.

After World War II, and particularly since the 1970s, many improvements to the practice of classical management have been proposed and adopted by organizations to varying degrees, for varying lengths of time, and with varying degrees of success. These and other methods to impose reason and new habits of thought and action on leaders have mostly fallen into the category of fads, whether it deserved or not, and further demonstrates the truth of Professor Haber's analysis. The more substantive, enterprise-wide systems for improving leadership and management practice include:

- Total Quality Management
- Business Process Reengineering
- Six Sigma
- Lean Six Sigma
- Lean Management

The proponents of each system or method, which relied on the use of scientific thinking, assumed that top leaders are predominately rational thinkers, that their principal job is to create wealth, and that they have a strong desire for more efficient work processes throughout the organization. But, over the decades, each new wave of proponents learned something different. They learned that irrational thinking is valued by leaders ("gut instinct" or intuition), power is as important or more important than wealth creation, and that efficient work processes are not a primary determinant of business or personal success. Despite learning this, little adjustment has been made in how progressive management is marketed to leaders. Leaders, of course, are not bad people. As the previous chapters illustrate, leaders must function in institutions that require a substantial amount of illogical thinking, far more than the people who proffer ameliorative solutions recognize.

The truth of this is self-evident if one considers how people think about their boss (see Table 2-2). They generally dislike bosses for various reasons, especially the exercise of arbitrary power and irrational thinking that directly affects their work or livelihood. An antidote to this is to become your own boss. Then, you too can enjoy the great pleasures of exercising arbitrary power and irrational thinking as circumstances dictate. Or, you can try to do better if you are able to surmount the restrictions imposed by the institutions of business and leadership. It is possible to do so, but most leaders are unable. This is due to a lack of training and education in the mindset and practices that must be diligently applied to generate a new institution of leadership that can function within the existing institution of business.

Lean management [5, 6] is the current system proffered to impose rational, scientific thinking and new habits of thought and action on leaders. Lean management is a simplified, derivative version of Toyota's management system [7-9]. Toyota's management system came under sustained study since the 1970s because of their success. Yet the real story is Toyota senior management's long-term commitment to running the business according to the facts (*de facto*) rather than by right (*de jure*) – not perfectly so, but good enough to be worth careful study, which led to many publications and the teaching of Toyota people's thinking and methods. The mindset, methods, and tools were developed and improved over several decades, some borrowed from Taylor's industrial engineering, that make people face reality so that the facts cannot be avoided, and action taken quickly based on the facts. This applies to all levels of the organization, from worker to president. People who are willing to learn Toyota's ways – to abandon their numerous preconceptions and learn new habits of thought and action – are amply rewarded intellectually and for the copious practical things they learn about how to improve processes and how to make a better world.

Prior to the term "Lean" being introduced in 1988, a loose association of academics, consultants, and trainers worked to inform business leaders and professional staff of the many virtues of Toyota's management system. For some, this work became a small business while for others it was extra income (e.g. book royalties) and the satisfaction of educating people, developing their skills, and improving work processes. All believed in their mission to advance the practices of leadership and management using Toyota's leadership and management methods as the guiding light. Any new and worthwhile idea has a certain amount of idealism attached to it, and that still exists today. Whether one promotes Toyota's management system or Lean management, there is a strong belief in the correctness of one's work. They are sure of this because they possess the facts of the matter. Yet, as we know, facts may be neither shared nor convincing.

By the mid-1990s, as Lean management transitioned from being small business to being bigger business, it came more fully under the priorities of the institutions of business and leadership regardless of whether it was for-profit or not-for-profit. The Lean movement has long had a self-interested goal shared by nearly every business: growth. It was globalized more than a decade ago and continuously seeks to penetrate new industries to generate sales and gain enthusiastic adherents. This, despite a fundamental problem – leaders resist or reject Lean management – that has only recently been elucidated [4]. The leaders of the Lean movement gave up on business leaders long ago. Instead, they decided to put their faith in workers, primarily professional staff, to help transform classically managed organizations into Lean organizations. They sought to create an alliance of "Lean workers of the world." Engineers would play an important but not exclusive role. Lean welcomes anyone who wants to learn how to improve processes and has the drive to make improvements by eliminating waste, unevenness, and unreasonableness.

The professional staff had the added task of figuring out how to engage leaders at the top of the organization and workers at the bottom, both of whom were more-or-less satisfied with the status quo and each possessing the power to say "no." Growth in the Lean movement meant quantity over quality. While legions of professionals have been trained in Lean thinking principles and practices, few have been able to affect comprehensive change. This is due in small part to the emergence over time of a great variation in understanding Lean principles and practices and confusion between that and Toyota's management system principles and practices. While dilution of Toyota's management system widened acceptance for Lean, acceptance of Lean management widened its dilution. Often, what people claim as Lean is unrecognizable as such.

Additionally, a global alliance of professional staff trained in Lean management means little if there exists fundamental antagonism in how leaders, professional staff, and workers view one another. Despite this, there are some excellent examples of organizations that have overcome these problems and achieved noteworthy measures of success. They span government, industry, and non-profits. However, successful examples remain few in relation to the huge number of organizations that exist world-wide. Furthermore, success must contend with that which leads to failure. Lean management, embodying such a different way to thinking and doing things, is susceptible to quick reversal to classical management when there are changes in top managers or company ownership [10]. The former being 100 percent likely while the latter, over the long run, is close to that same number.

The more typical outcome for Lean management adopted by organizations paralleled that which occurred in the days of Scientific Management. Leaders felt that the only changes necessary were to the work that workers (non-management staff and laborers) do. Leaders accepted the use of certain Lean methods and tools to improve processes in production and non-production work. The institutions of business and leadership, including preconceptions about business and leadership, assured that improvement work would be bureaucratized and surveilled in ways to as to limit their impact to narrow business objectives such as productivity improvement and cost reduction. This approach resulted in attainment of only a small fraction of the available productivity improvement and cost reduction, but that was good enough.

These phenomena did not capture the attention of Lean movement leaders in any significant way. Instead, efforts were invested into doing more of what had been done in the past and offering shifting definitions of Lean and shifting explanations of what Lean was to further expand interest: a production system, a management system, a strategy, a learning method, an educational system, etc. Failing to learn the lessons of the past, the Lean movement was unprepared and seems unwilling to accept that Lean management has, for the most part, been subsumed by the old classical management.

In sum, the effort to create a global alliance of professional staff trained in Lean management – "Lean workers of the world" – has been thwarted (thus far) by the institutions of business and leadership, and also by the institution of workmanship wherein workers (laborers) also seek to maintain the status quo. Importantly, the Lean movement has been unable to convince the public at-large (society) of the merits of Lean management as a replacement for classical management, or the need for changes to the institutions of business and leadership – notwithstanding constant and concerted efforts made by many people and organizations to make sure that changes to the institutions of business and leadership do not occur. Ameliorative countermeasures to classical management and the institutions of business and leadership began with Scientific Management and progressed to Total Quality Management, Six Sigma, and Lean management. Each of these movements succumbed to common irrationalities that eventually undercut that which they sought to achieve. Lean movement leaders' strategies, tactics, and goals for promoting and gaining acceptance for Lean management have been largely the same for decades. This is irrational on its face given the realities described previously in this volume, and demonstrates that logical, fact-based Lean thinkers also make use of big doses of illogical thinking for sense-making and survival just as any business leader does.

The outside view, being largely inoperative for decades, compromises the credibility of Lean management and the Lean movement. The critical self-analysis that existed within the Scientific Management movement functions much less effectively within the Lean movement. There are occasional mild admissions of difficulty rather than deep thinking about what went wrong. At some point, one would expect that the time will come when resources expended to grow sales and the number of ardent Lean followers no longer provides an adequate return, leading to a major change in focus, direction, alliance, or dissolution. In business, dissolution is often the most profitable route.

Lean management, following from Toyota's management system, has its own aesthetic judgments of beauty and ugliness. Generally, they are the opposite of that described in Chapter 2. The behaviors judged to be beautiful by leaders, informed by reason (cause-and-effect), are in close alignment with the leadership behaviors judged to be beautiful by workers, as shown in Table 3-1. This is because there is a recognition that people (all stakeholders) must be treated with respect for teamwork to occur and be effective. Respect is beautiful. Further, it is recognized that disrespect generates waste, unevenness, and unreasonableness, which consumes valuable resources. Waste, unevenness, and unreasonableness are ugly. Time is a particularly important resource for businesses that operate in competitive markets. However, there is no ranking of the resources required for productive work; all are important, and none should be wasted. Processes must be continuously scrutinized for the existence of waste (problems) so that it can be eliminated.

Problems are an aesthetic that is considered beautiful in Lean management. No problem is ugly because there is no such thing as no problem. Problems always exist, though one may not yet be able to see them. What classical management considers as ugly (Figures 2-4, bottom; Figure 2-5; Figure 2-6, bottom), Lean management sees as beautiful – an opportunity to use one's intelligence to understand and solve problems. Problem-solving, at the root cause (vs. band-aid), is beautiful. So is the curiosity and drive to take action and solve problems with one's team. Improvement is also beautiful, but in recognition that it can be irregular. Meaning, two steps forward and one step back. It is unrealistic to think that improvement always proceeds as shown in Figure 2-3 (top) – either in uniformity or slope.

Lean management and classical management share a similar, but not the same view of beauty when it comes to alignment. In Lean, misalignment is management's fault, not workers' fault, and it signals the existence of problems that need to be examined in search of practical solutions

Table 3-1. Aesthetics of Leadership Behaviors

Beautiful Leadership Behaviors as Seen by Leaders	Beautiful Leadership Behaviors as Seen by Workers
Respect	Respect
Humility	Humility
Calmness	Calmness
Consistency	Consistency
Deliberation	Deliberation
Listening	Listening
Trust	Trust
Sharing	Sharing
Patient	Patient
Adaptive	Adaptive
Sincerity	Sincerity
Intelligence	Intelligence
Wisdom	Wisdom
Casual/Flexible	Casual/Flexible
Cooperation	Cooperation

(countermeasures, actually). Leaders' view of workers is that they are the ones doing the value-creating work (beauty), and who are encouraged to use their intelligence to think of creative, low-cost ways to improve the work. This is something that machines cannot yet do. Therefore, workers (beauty) are seen as valuable resources to develop rather than costs to eliminate as seen in classical management. Robots and automation are applied to work that is hazardous to humans or to assist humans (beauty), not used simply to replace labor wherever possible (ugly). The use of leverage is restricted and used sparingly, only when truly necessary, not routinely as used in classical management. Creating winners and losers leads to poor teamwork and generates waste, unevenness, and unreasonableness. Suppliers (beauty) are business partners with shared interests. They are valuable resources, so payment is prompt and other key resources are shared to improve cooperation and teamwork. Table 3-2 shows some examples of aesthetic judgments in Lean.

Table 3-2. Examples of Aesthetic Judgments in Lean

	Beautiful	Ugly
Sight	Workplace	Conference room
	Observation	Ignorance
	Working	Idleness
	Company uniform	Designer apparel
	Orderliness	Disorder
	Improvement	Status quo
	Flow	Stagnation
Sound	Questions	No questions
	Let's try it out	It's impossible
	We'll find a way	It won't work
	Keep thinking	We're done
	Let's work together	I have the answer
Object	Craftsmanship	Producing
	Quality	Defects
	Skilled	Unskilled
	One page	Many pages
Experience	Teamwork	Individualism
	Clarity	Confusion
	Curiosity	Disinterest
	Problems	No problems
	Thinking	Compliance
	Quick	Slow
	Relationships	Conflict

Running the business according to the facts (*de facto*) – scientific thinking in the forms of kaizen, PDSA, root cause analysis A3 reports – rather than by right (*de jure*) is astonishingly different and truly eye-opening to those who want to learn and lead people towards a better today and tomorrow (Table 3-2).

In sum, the aesthetics of Lean management, reflecting the aesthetics of Toyota management, makes judgments of beauty that are vastly different than the judgments of beauty in classical management. From this, we can see why Lean management struggles to gain acceptance among the top leaders of organizations. Indeed, no method has yet been found that can render as obsolete the aesthetic judgments of beauty in classical management. Irrationality, social habits of thought and action, and preconceptions are deeply embedded in classical management by way of classical and neoclassical economics. These leaders, confident personally and professionally, have little cause or reason to abandon their aesthetic judgments, many of which are connected to cherished traditions that bestow honor, status, and respectability. They easily recognize that Lean management is not the only path to success. Classical management gets the job done, if not by a mile then by an inch. That's good enough for most leaders, but likely not for society. The needs of society are more expansive and of greater human value than the narrow interests of individual leaders or the corporation.

The Lean movement has its own aesthetics. Table 3-3 shows some of its fundamental aesthetics. Perhaps most important are these three judgments of beauty: success, success stories, and enthusiasm, and their ugly corollaries, failure, failure stories, and critiques. While success stories illuminate what to do and how to do it, their inverse (what not to do and how not to do it) are inadequate for describing why people and organizations struggle or fail. This is the domain of analytical critique and formal failure analysis.

Table 3-3. Fundamental Aesthetics of the Lean Movement

Beautiful	Ugly
Success	Failure
Success stories	Failure stories
Enthusiasm	Critiques
Agreement	Dissent
Progress	Struggle
Learning	Speaks the jargon
Use Lean tools	Misunderstand Lean tools
Information sharing	Information hoarding
Classroom training	Shop floor training

Lean management is a product that is marketed and sold according to the common methods used by business. This includes conferences, workshop, training, consulting, books, webinars, social media (Twitter, Facebook, LinkedIn), Internet advertising, direct mail, blogs, etc. It is big business in its own small way. Consequently, there is little appetite for failure, failure stories, failure analysis, and critiques

These are intrinsically ugly and extrinsically ugly because they are bad for business and personal reputations. Sales and status will be negatively impacted. The people and organizations who have strong positions in the marketplace do not want the brand identity to be contaminated by the facts. Lean movement social habits of thought and action, as well as preconceptions specific to the Lean movement, reflect the restrictions imposed by the institutions of business and leadership. These influence the business of Lean just as they influence any other business.

Solutions are not easily found, and, if problems are solved by others external to the coterie of socially acknowledged experts, it is unlikely solutions would be adopted due to the pervasive social habit in business of ignoring ideas from the outside – commonly known as the "not invented here syndrome." The strong bias against outside ideas reveals two points of hypocrisy:

1. The devotion of Lean people to Dr. W. Edwards Deming's philosophy, inclusive of the necessity of outside views for making progress.
2. The professed importance of facts, truth, and problem-solving.

Consequently, only certain outside views are welcome (success, success stories, and enthusiasm), and only certain problems are welcomed as worthy to be recognized and worked on towards their solution (not failure, failure stories, and critiques). Barring any change in aesthetics, those judged as beautiful in Table 3-3 will dictate the future trajectory of the Lean movement.

The pretense of integrity and the irrationality of the Lean movement makes it more difficult to impose rationality on the irrational institutions of business and leadership. The top leaders of classically managed organizations surely see this. Furthermore, it is likely they have long seen Lean management as something interesting but that which is not useful for formulating pragmatic (expedient and opportunistic; "instrumental rationality") solutions to common business problems. Despite this, the Lean movement continues to seek new individual and corporate customers, perhaps knowing that it offers little actual value in exchange for its goods and services. If so, the Lean movement is parasitic in the sense of being mildly detrimental to business in its extraction of fees, selling of hope, and unwillingness to tackle its own biggest problems.

What started out three decades ago as a method for improving management and leadership practice in organizations became a business that often does not follow its own advice. The endless boosterism of Lean management shows that it has been contaminated by the institutions of business and leadership, and, in the view of many, has descended into hucksterism. This is unfortunate. But could things have been done any different 30 or 40 years ago? In hindsight, yes. The strategies, goals, and objectives of the Scientific Management movement should have been studied much more carefully. Likewise, the documentary record of business leaders' response to Scientific Management, and other contemporaneous written works, should have been studied very closely. This would have begun the lengthy process of learning both who and what Lean management was up against. Would it have made a difference? That is impossible to say. But without doubt, understanding the problem in detail – why leaders resist or reject progressive management – would have uncovered many creative solutions to try. A breakthrough might have occurred, or all ideas might have been easily quashed by the institutions of business and leadership, thereby perpetuating classical management and the many benefits that it affords to leaders.

In addition, we must always keep in mind that leaders eagerly pursue machine technology to increase productivity, lower costs, and increase profits. That is the social habit of thought and action. Leaders are averse to pursuing new technologies that compete with their power and authority – meaning, *new management technologies* such as Toyota's management system or Lean management. Machines do not compete with or weaken leaders' interests, but new management technologies do. One can think of the institutions of business and leadership as a large, opaque canopy that blocks out the sun and prevents anything from growing beneath it, thereby maintaining the status quo.

The dominant nature of these two institutions make for a very difficult, but not impossible, challenge. Progress will be made as we improve our understanding of how the institutions of business and leadership function to perpetuate the status quo. These institutions are not perfect; they contain weaknesses that can be exploited when the time is right. This book, together with *The Triumph of Classical Management*, provides comprehensive analyses of how business leaders react and respond to progressive management that was previously unknown by Lean movement leaders or their most insightful peers. However, I am not optimistic that current or future leaders of the Lean movement will make use of this information for reasons previously cited. Lean is, after all, a business, and business leaders can be quite irrational at times. The value of these books will likely be the outside view that they offer to someone or something else.

Questions to Reflect On

- Is it possible to change the common leadership habit of thought that winning by an inch is good enough?

- Do you agree that the business of Lean needs improvement? If so, how would you improve it?

- The professional staff ("Lean workers of the world") have largely failed to engage leaders. What can they do to close implicit or explicit gaps in interest (i.e. progress vs. status quo) with workers? Could an alliance between the two succeed in putting pressure on leaders to adopt Lean management? What ideas would you try?

- What could the Lean movement do to convince the public at-large (nationally) of the merits of Lean management as a worthy and necessary replacement for classical management?

- Examine Tables 3-2 and 3-3. Can you identify other aesthetics associated with Lean management and the Lean movement?

References

[1] Taylor, F.W. (1911), *Principles of Scientific Management*, Harper and Brothers, New York, NY, page 7

[2] Ibid, p. 140

[3] Haber, S. (1964), *Efficiency and Uplift Scientific Management in the Progressive Era 1890-1920*, University of Chicago Press, Chicago, Illinois, pp. 16-17

[4] Emiliani, B. (2018), *The Triumph of Classical Management Over Lean Management: How Tradition Prevails and What to Do About It*, Cubic, LLC, South Kingstown, Rhode Island

[5] Womack, J., Jones, D., and Roos, D. (1990), *The Machine that Changed the World*, Rawson Associates, New York, NY

[6] Womack, J. and Jones, D. (1996), *Lean Thinking: Banish Waste and Create Wealth in Your Corporation*, Simon & Schuster, New York, NY

[7] Ohno, T. (1988), *Toyota Production System – Beyond Large-Scale Production*, Productivity Press, Portland, Oregon

[8] Monden, Y. (1983), *Toyota Production System: Practical Approach to Production Management*, Engineering and Management Press, Norcross, Georgia

[9] Liker, J. (2004), *The Toyota Way*, McGraw-Hill, New York, NY.

[10] Emiliani, B. *et al.* (2007), *Better Thinking, Better Results: Case Study and Analysis of an Enterprise-Wide Lean Transformation*, second edition, The CLBM, LLC, Wethersfield, Conn.

4

Conclusion

ir·ra·tion·al *adj* 1. not logical or reasonable

in·sti·tu·tion *n* 1. social habits of thought and action

"The outcome of any serious research can only be to make two questions grow where only one grew before."

- Thorstein Veblen

For more than a century people have speculated why business leaders resist or reject new systems of progressive management. The first comprehensive analysis of this problem appeared in the book *The Triumph of Classical Management Over Lean Management.* This volume examined the problem from a different direction (Figure P-2) using two new analytical methods. It explored how irrationality functions within the institutions of business and leadership, and the Lean movement, and how social habits of thought and action that produce these institutions thwart efforts to impose rationality in leadership and management practice. The book also critiqued the aesthetics of the institution of leadership and the Lean movement and described how their aesthetics function as powerful mechanisms to maintain the status quo despite the obvious need for change.

The analytical methods used in each book have produced sobering realities that many would prefer not to confront. But we must confront them if we hope to make progress when progress needs to be made. The function of economics as defined by Enlightenment philosophers and classical and neoclassical economists, is production, distribution, and consumption. It is an economics based on producer-to-consumer. The *form* that follows from the *function* is batch-and-queue material and information processing (classical management) and the associated institutions of business and leadership. In an economics based on consumer-to-producer, as in Toyota's management system and Lean management, a different *form* follows from the same *function*, material and information flow. This results in a different institution of leadership that can operate successfully within the irrationalities and restrictions imposed by the institution of business. However, the weight of history, philosophy, and business practice retard these new forms from growing and improving and correcting or replacing the old forms.

The institutions of business and leadership are emotionally unintelligent, irrational, and inconsistent, resulting in promiscuous behaviors that are forever in search of the best deal at any moment in time, guided by self-interest. The tangled scribble illustrations on the front and back covers of this book depict the chaotic search for the best deal. At any point in time (location on the line), the tangent vector points towards a sensible direction (decision). But over time, as leaders change, as mistakes are repeated, and as reason inevitably traces its own circle, mere change becomes synonymous with progress. The adage "the more things change, the more they stay the same" attests to the inaccurate correlation that change is synonymous with progress.

To make real progress in relation to actual social needs, one must accept the existence of bad management. To accept bad management requires accepting the existence of bad leadership. Accepting bad leadership means to accept bad thinking and bad decision-making. This cascade of ugliness and dishonor is repugnant to leaders. If we comprehend business as a political, not economic, organization, then it is easy to understand how irrational thinking and the preservation of the status quo are of great importance and necessary for survival. Because intelligence (critical thinking) is the enemy of the status quo, people must be duped every day into believing that what is is the best there is; that nothing better can be achieved without massive costs and disruptions. Predictions made with the intent to frighten people and motivate their retreat to the comfort of the status quo are no accident. Absent voluntary change, leaders may eventually be forced into changing the institutions of business and leadership. This may come about through consumer action (boycott), legal action, or the recognition of life-changing pressures such as climate change, disease, or some form of war. The static aesthetic judgments of beauty will someday meet one or more formidable challenges.

It is instructive to comprehend where we now are and how far we must go. Emiel van Est wrote a blog post that included an image depicting "The Leadership Gap" [1] (go to the blog post to see the original image in color). With his permission, the image is shown on the following page. In Figure C-1, Mr. van Est creatively fuses ideas from the books *Spiral Dynamics* [2] and *The Triumph of Classical Management Over Lean Management* [3], as well as Figure P-1. As his image shows, there is a large gap between classical leadership (Dominance Paradigm) and the required leadership for the 21st century and beyond (Symbiotic Paradigm). As each past innovator of progressive management has learned, it is an almost unimaginable step simply to move from the Dominance Paradigm (*de jure*) to the Control Paradigm (*de facto*), let alone the Involvement Paradigm or the Symbiotic Paradigm. We remain stuck in the Dominance Paradigm. Classical management and its

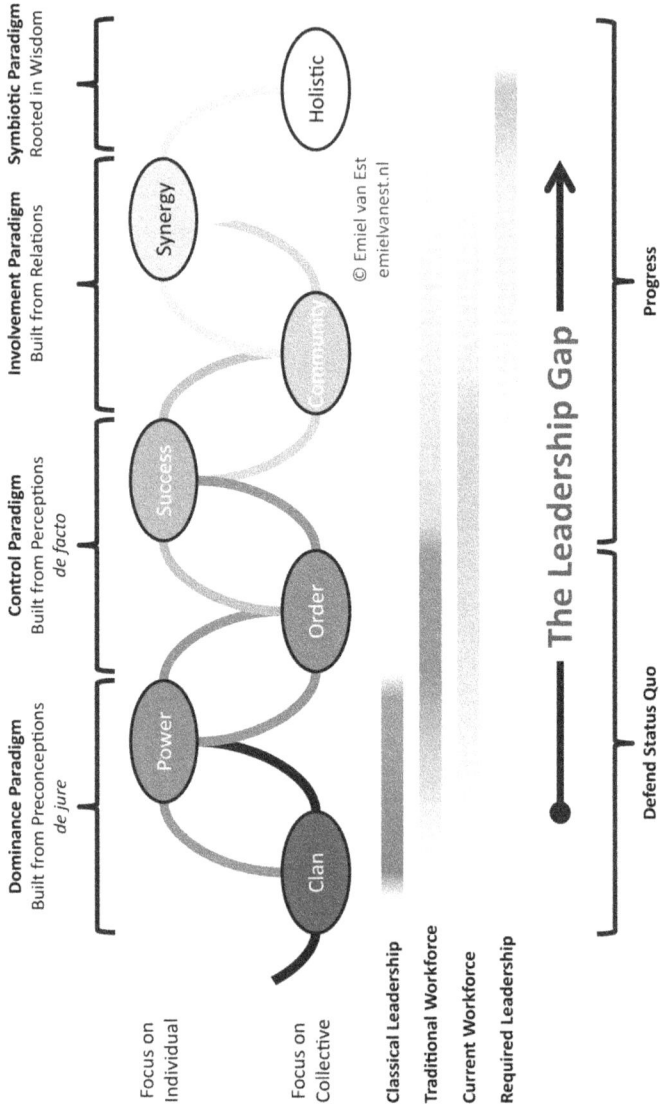

Figure C-1. The gap between classical leadership (left side) and the leadership required for a sustainable future (right side).
Source: Emiel van Est. Used with permission.

institutions of business and leadership assume that time is a resource that can be freely wasted, as it has been since the dawn of big business the 1880s and the introduction of Scientific Management soon thereafter. The profligate wasting of time spent preserving institutions at the expense of society's interests is breathtaking. For all that the institutions of business and leadership have given to humanity in the past, they have much more to offer in the future if they can be brought forward to the times we now live in. This will contribute greatly to improving the human condition and allow people to lead more prosperous and satisfying lives.

Irrationality may be a useful survival mechanism for these institutions, but it is likely less so as a survival mechanism for humanity. The combination of logic and illogic used to assure survival in the past will likely not be useful for survival in the future. A different combination of logic and illogic are needed. The institutions of business and leadership and their suffocating aesthetics also illustrate how far behind we are and how far we have to go. Yet, neither leaders nor society may see the need. The aesthetic judgments of beauty remain overpowering.

Let's assume influential business and political leaders will soon have the resolve to initiate change for the better from above and make the case to society below that adjustments must be made. Because the desired ends are unknowable, the required course of action should be trial-and-error, rapidly incorporating feedback into each subsequent round of trail-and-error, one step at a time. There is a risk that incrementalism under the current system that created the need for change will result in the marshalling of forces to extinguish change. Trial-and-error will, of necessity, disturb the institutions of business and leadership and alter their aesthetic judgments of beauty. It will be difficult to do this in ways that people recognize as not causing harm to themselves or others. Perhaps they can be taught that ugliness is merely a problem, one that initiates curiosity to understand the true nature of the problem and identify countermeasures to put into place so that the problem does not recur. If the problem does recur, the process of recognizing the problem, understanding its root causes, and identifying countermeasures begins anew. That's progress.

Returning to the aesthetics of the institutions of business, leadership, and the Lean movement described in Chapter 3, it is apparent that the Lean movement cannot yet claim a superior position. All three institutions operate on malfunctioning aesthetics. This explains the more-or-less continuous existence of large gaps between plans and the actual results. With respect to the Lean movement, the plan was that countless top leaders would accept the rational arguments for adopting a new management system. Organizations of all sizes would rush to transform from classical management to Lean management and achieve success akin to Toyota to the benefit of all stakeholders. That did not happen.

Figure C-2 illustrates how the gap between plan and actual leads to a decision about how to solve problems. The left side is the irrational path for problem-solving that produces

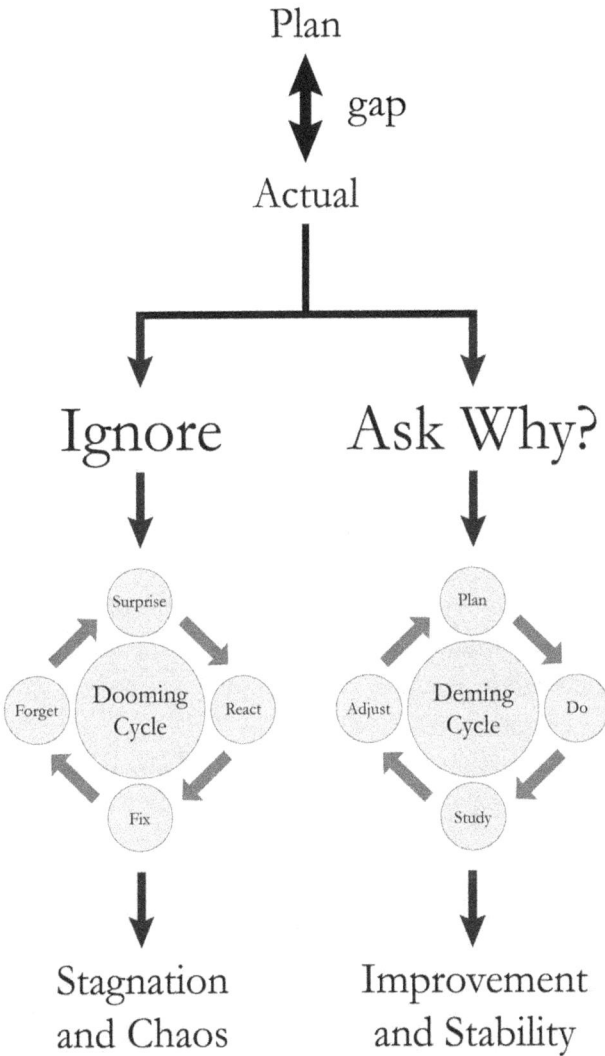

Figure C-2. The Dooming cycle and the Deming cycle.

perpetual difficulties (Dooming cycle), while the right side is the rational path for problem-solving that produces perpetual improvement (Deming cycle). In truth, both sides contain irrationality, the Dooming cycle containing more irrationality than the Deming cycle. One can safely say that well-placed irrationality exists more on the right side (Ask Why?) than on the left side (Ignore). Well-placed irrationality is conducive to progress.

The aesthetic judgments of beauty associated with each path could not be more different. Tables 3-1 and 3-2 reveal the craftsmanship (workmanship) that is fundamental to Lean management, from worker to CEO. These aesthetics do not exist in classical management. The aesthetics of classical management shown in the Tables and Figures in Chapter 2 reveal a built-in lack of skill and ability. The aesthetics of the institutions of business and leadership and the Lean movement convey and reinforce political messages rather than the importance of good thinking, good workmanship, and good products and services.

The points of analysis in this book were the institutions of business and leadership, as well as the Lean movement. It explored the *social habits of thought and action that are irrational.* Because these are brought to life through our leaders, there are some questions that only leaders can answer. These include:

- What type of shared existence do leaders want to create in organizations (i.e. wide or narrow *de jure-de facto* gap) and what effects do they want business to have on society?
- Are leaders motivated to correct and improve the institutions of business and leadership as

time and needs dictate (Figures P-1 and C-1), or do they prefer business as usual?

- Will leaders remain on the path established 500 years ago (and earlier), or will they accept a slightly higher purpose and slightly more rational moral direction?

- What is the role of Lean management and the Lean movement? Do they remain central to making human progress, or have they become peripheral to it?

- Has the confluence of progressive Lean ideas, the spirit of the times, and the interests of business leaders that are needed to affect change passed or is it yet to come?

Finally, I am always interested to hear from readers because I learn new things. Tell me what you think of this book or let's make arrangements to have a conversation by phone or Skype. You pick the topic. Contact me at bob@bobemiliani.com.

Questions to Reflect On

- Lean management seems ill-suited for the times we now live in, an era of individualism, flood of daily distractions (e.g. social media, cell phone alerts), authoritarian leadership, alternative facts, social and political tumult, etc. How do you create conditions for greater rationality so that appeals to leaders' intelligence (or well-placed irrationality) for adopting Lean management are more successful?

- Is it fundamentally too much to ask of progressive Lean management to correct irrationality and the institutions of business and leadership for anything more than a small number of organizations? Why?

- What did you learn from the Introduction, Chapter 1, Chapter 2, and Chapter 3? Make a list enumerating how each of the four parts of the book: a) changed your thinking, b) triggered new ideas, and c) the ways in which you can apply what you learned.

- Read Emiel van Est's blog post. He poses interesting question regarding Figure C-1: Why do we have the leaders we have? Because many of us chose to follow them. So who do you follow and why?

- What aspects of this book do you like or agree with, or dislike or disagree with?

References

[1] van Est, E. (2019), "The Leadership Gap," blog post, 28 December,   https://www.emielvanest.nl/the-leadership-gap/, accessed 29 December

[2] Beck D. and Cowan C. (1996), *Spiral Dynamics: Mastering Values, Leadership, and Change*," Blackwell Publishing, Oxford, England

[3] Emiliani, B. (2018), *The Triumph of Classical Management Over Lean Management: How Tradition Prevails and What to Do About It*, Cubic, LLC, South Kingstown, Rhode Island

A New Economics for Business Leaders

Some Assumptions in Classical and Neoclassical Economics

Static, equilibrium conditions
Individual
Rational behavior
Price = cost + profit
Predetermined outcomes
Utility
Profit maximization
Availability of full information
Self-interest (person)
Surviving the present
Acceptance of waste
Money focus
Incurious (recognize effects)
Pecuniary (money) interest
Action based on preconceptions
Leader mindset: metaphysical realism
Social benefits derived from self-interest

Producer-Focused Batch-and-Queue Production
(asynchronous supply and demand)

The parts that **do evolve** are those which define the need for equilibrium.

Some Assumptions in Toyota Economics

Dynamic, change, evolution
Team
Ideas and creativity
Price - cost = profit
Outcomes by trial-and-error
Value
Cost reduction
Availability of partial information
Community interest (humanity)
Surviving the future
Rejection of waste
Process focus
Curious (cause-and-effect)
Balance of interests
Action based on perceptions
Leader mindset: physical pragmatism
Social benefits derived from teamwork

Customer-Focused Flow Production
(synchronous supply and demand)

The parts that **do not evolve** are those which define the need for evolution.

NOTES

NOTES

About the Author

M.L. "Bob" Emiliani is a professor in the School of Engineering, Science, and Technology at Connecticut State University in New Britain, Conn., where he teaches a course on leadership, a unique course that analyzes failures in management decision-making, as well as other courses.

Bob earned a Bachelor of Science degree in mechanical engineering from the University of Miami, a Master of Science degree in chemical engineering from the University of Rhode Island, and a Doctor of Philosophy degree in Engineering from Brown University.

He worked in the consumer products and aerospace industries for 15 years, beginning as a materials engineer. He has held management positions in engineering, manufacturing, and supply chain management at Pratt & Whitney.

Bob joined academia in September 1999. While in academia, he developed the Lean teaching pedagogy and led activities to continuously improve master's degree programs.

Emiliani has authored or co-authored 21 books, four book chapters, and more than 45 peer-reviewed papers. He has received six awards for writing.

Please visit www.bobemiliani.com